MW00560822

Quilt Block Genius

Over 300 Pieced Quilt Blocks to Make 1001 Blocks with No Math Charts

EXPANDED SECOND EDITION

by Sue Voegtlin

Landauer Publishing

Quilt Block Genius EXPANDED SECOND EDITION

Landauer Publishing (*www.landauerpub.com*) is an imprint of
Fox Chapel Publishing Company, Inc.

Copyright © 2020 by Sue Voegtlin and Fox Chapel Publishing Company,
Inc., 903 Square Street, Mount Joy, PA 17552.

Project Team:
Editors: Laurel Albright/Sue Voegtlin
Copy Editor: Katie Ocasio
Designer: Laurel Albright
Photographer: Sue Voegtlin

ISBN: 978-1-947163-18-8

All rights reserved. No part of this book may be reproduced, stored
in a retrieval system, or transmitted in any form or by any means,
electronic, mechanical, photocopying, recording, or otherwise, without
the prior written permission of Fox Chapel Publishing, except for
the inclusion of brief quotations in an acknowledged review and the
enlargement of the template patterns in this book for personal use only.
The patterns themselves, however, are not to be duplicated for resale or
distribution under any circumstances. Any such copying is a violation of
copyright law.

Note to Professional Copy Services:
The publisher grants you permission to make up to ten copies for any
purchaser of this book who states the copies are for personal use.

Library of Congress Control Number: 2019950546

We are always looking for talented authors. To submit an idea,
please send a brief inquiry to acquisitions@foxchapelpublishing.com.

Printed in China

24 23 22 21   2 4 6 8 10 9 7 5 3

This book has been published with the intent to provide accurate and
authoritative information in regard to the subject matter within. While
every precaution has been taken in the preparation of this book, the
author and publisher expressly disclaim any responsibility for any errors,
omissions, or adverse effects arising from the use or application of the
information contained herein.

Contents

Foreword

Content from the original *Block Genius* is here with all 201 pieced blocks with No Math charts. I've added a new finished size of 4½" to 6, 9, and 12-inch finished blocks. Quilters who like to make mini quilts, or want to make sampler quilts like Dear Jane or Civil War replicas, have 201 blocks to choose from with the math done for those beautiful, little blocks.

I've added 100 blocks in 3 new grid sizes, 5 x 5, 7 x 7 and 8 x 8, each with 3 finished block sizes, and no math charts. While not as versatile as the sizes in the first book, the new block sizes double and triple, giving you a whole new range of small to large blocks. Quilts can be just as dramatic using 14", 15", or 16" finished sizes. Or make a sampler quilt using multiple sizes of blocks.

Be sure to read through the front of the book before making your blocks, especially if you are a beginner or you are new to piecing. The information there is extensive, instructions are easy to follow, and you may refer to techniques in other projects as you start piecing your own blocks.

I've designed over fifty blocks for the new sizes. It was my goal after writing the first book to design my own, and I'm happy to share them with you. You should try it! Choose a traditional block and take away or move pieces around. It will allow you to see how a block can evolve into a design of your own. Draw a grid on graph paper, get out your colored pencils and create a block with your favorite colors. Use the math charts and apply the measurements to your design. It's all here; no need for a calculator!

Quilt Block Genius includes 300 blocks in over 1000 sizes with the math done for you. That's a lot of information and inspiration! Choose a block, choose your favorite colors, and choose a size. The possibilities are endless.

Sue Voegtlin,
Des Moines, Iowa

Pick a Block...

...any block. Construct it as you see it or change the colors to make it your own. I wrote instructions for the blocks in this book based on the No Math Block Charts, pages 202–203. It's a perfect reference when you decide to make blocks you don't find here, or if you are ready to design your own. Step out of the box! Color outside the lines! Create your own beautiful blocks!

Introduction to the Genius of the Grid System

Blocks can be made in many sizes but 6, 9, and 12-inch blocks are some of the most used by quilters. Their versatility makes them fit easily into 2 x 2, 3 x 3, 4 x 4, and 6 x 6 grids.

Incremental measurements for cutting block components are included on most quilting rulers making it easy to rotary cut pieces. No piece will have anything less than an ⅛" (0.32cm) increment.

There are so many great resources for block designs, including books, internet resources, and vintage quilts. Most of the blocks, other than a few my friend Laurel and I designed, are over 100 years old. They have certainly stood the test of time.

I tried to correctly identify each block by name. But some had identical names but a different design or colorway. Flipping or turning a component can change a name and create a new block.

Take a look at Jacob's Ladder, page 143, and Wagon Tracks, page 150. The cutting instructions and components are the same. It's a perfect example of how orientation of a part and changing a color will change a block name.

Grids and Block Structure

Most quilt blocks are designed by using a base grid of squares. A grid is based on how a block is divided on two sides. The squares within the grid are all the same size. Below are the seven grids used to make the blocks in this book.

2 x 2

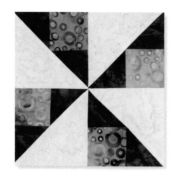

(2 grid or
4 patch)

3 x 3

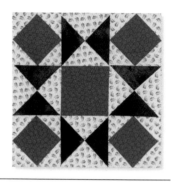

(3 grid or
9 patch)

4 x 4

(4 grid; part of 2 grid
block family)

5 x 5

(5 grid category)

6 x 6

(6 grid; part of 3 grid
block family)

7 x 7

(7 grid category)

8 x 8

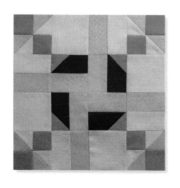

(8 grid; part of 2 grid
block family)

The Parts

Each square within the grid can be divided to create more pattern in the block. With each division, we can start to see other components besides squares; half- and quarter-square triangles, flying geese, or a square-in-a-square.

Cutting Charts

In the block section, you'll see a photograph of each block, and cutting instructions with icons representing the pieces you will cut and subcut. Seam allowances are included in the measurements given for making 6, 9, and 12-inch finished blocks. All measurements are exact; there will be no trimming except for fabric "tails."

Colors are represented by letters with "A" being the lightest and "B, C, and D," representing medium to dark values. You can change your color choices based on these values and you will maintain the same look of the block.

An illustration of how the block is constructed is shown below the cutting chart. Instructions for piecing the components that make up the block are referenced by page number below the illustration.

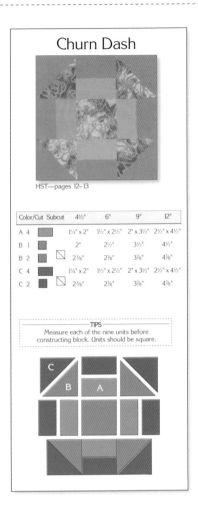

Churn Dash

HST—pages 12–13

Color/Cut	Subcut	4½"	6"	9"	12"
A 4		1¼" x 2"	1½" x 2½"	2" x 3½"	2½" x 4½"
B 1		2"	2½"	3½"	4½"
B 2		2⅜"	2⅞"	3⅞"	4⅞"
C 4		1¼" x 2"	1½" x 2½"	2" x 3½"	2½" x 4½"
C 2		2⅜"	2⅞"	3⅞"	4⅞"

TIPS
Measure each of the nine units before constructing block. Units should be square.

Good to Know

After I cut all the pieces for a block, I laid them out beside my sewing machine, or on my ironing board, so I could sew the parts together in order. I liked being able to have a visual of the block instead of all the pieces sitting in piles in front of me. It saved time, too.

To Pin or not to Pin

For me, there is no cut and dried rule when it comes to using pins. I keep them handy but pick and choose when I use them. Since I was working with smaller pieces, I didn't pin every time I sewed. I tended to use pins more when I was sewing bias cut pieces and when I sewed segments together to construct a block. That way, my seams matched and my pieces stayed aligned. If you are a beginner, I suggest using pins more often than not. There is nothing I want more than for you to have a satisfying experience as you begin your block and quiltmaking journey!

Sewing Small Pieces

I discovered I was getting some wonkiness on some pieces because I couldn't hold on to them past my sewing machine foot. I found a stiletto came in handy when I got to the end of a seam. I could use the point to hold the pieces in line at the finish. But read on... leaders and enders can help, too.

Good to Know

If you need to undo your stitching, avoid pulling apart; you will resize pieces quicker than you realize by stretching the fabric. Using your ripping tool, lay your sewn piece flat, and cut every third or fourth stitch. Remove any thread and gently re-press before sewing.

Cutting

I liked my 3½" (8.89cm) and 4½" x 12½"
(11.43 x 31.75cm) rulers, and my 6½" (16.51cm)
square ruler, all with ⅛" increments. Because the
fabric pieces were smaller, the rulers were easier
to handle. Hold onto your rulers when you cut. The
grippers on the back of mine didn't work as well
with smaller pieces of fabric so applying a little more
pressure was necessary when cutting.

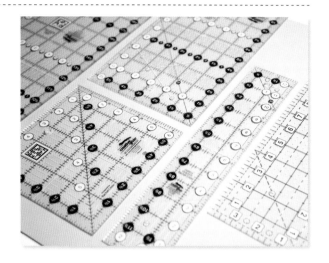

Quarter-Inch Seams

The cutting instructions include seam allowances, which is
part of the "genius" feature. The math is done for you! It
is important to sew accurate ¼" (0.64cm) seams. Being off
just a thread or two adds up as you sew, either increasing or
decreasing the size of your block.

I used my quarter-inch foot and extended the "line" with a
piece of painter's tape taped to the throat of my machine.
Use the tools that work best for you. Consistency is the key
to accurate piecing. Switching from one machine to another,
or switching out your tool of choice can make a huge difference
in the way your blocks come together.

It's a good idea to sew a sample quarter-inch seam. Check
the accuracy with whichever technique you choose and make
adjustments accordingly.

Leader and Ender Scraps

Sewing small pieces can be tricky when you begin your
seam, especially if you are starting on the tip of a triangle.
To keep the fabric from getting pulled down into the needle
plate, use a small scrap of fabric, the "leader," followed by
your pieces. When you come to the end of your seam, use
another scrap, the "ender," stitch into it, and leave it under
your machine foot. The ender has now become the leader
for the next seam. Snip threads that connect your pieces to
these scraps.

Cutting; Quarter-Inch Seams; Leader and Ender Scraps

Pressing

I don't necessarily follow the standard for pressing seams. Because I was only making one block at a time, I pressed my seams open so the block would lay flat.

I understand the concept of pressing seams toward the darker fabric. I think this is important, especially if you are sewing light and dark fabrics together. If you choose to press the seams to the dark side, try this: Lay your sewn piece dark side up, open it, and press. The seams will automatically press to the dark side. (Finger pressing is a nice "assist" to get started with your iron.)

Take great care as you press the pieces of your block. I do believe in the "press, don't iron" rule. Lift your iron up and down instead of "ironing" from side to side. Steam or no steam? Again, it's a personal preference. I like a little bit but I also know I accidentally stretched my pieces more than I anticipated using steam. This is an instance where I knew better but I just had to do it my way. I paid the price with some time consuming do-overs!

Good to Know

When I finished a block, I did a last press with spray starch. It gives the block some additional stability. I sprayed the back of the block to make sure my seams stayed open, too.

Color

Making one block at a time gave me the opportunity to play around with color. It's a great way to use your scraps and stash. If you find a color combination you love and a block pattern you really like, then you have started the design process for an entire quilt.

I think color is a very personal thing. I like finding one color or fabric pattern and building from it. Use photos, paint chips, or a fabric collection as inspiration. And don't forget the color wheel. The science and theory represented in it is a surefire way to make your color choices theoretically correct and most appealing to the eye. Pick your favorite color on the wheel and try using the colors across and next to it. BUT, don't be afraid to experiment.

If you look at the blocks in this book, and you aren't crazy about my color choices, think about how you would change them to reflect your own preferences. This is the time to teach yourself how to look beyond what you see. Make a quick line sketch of the block if it helps to see the block without color. You can use grid paper if you want to be really exact. Use your colored pencils or markers to play around with your own colorways.

Getting Started

Step-by-Step

You might be inclined to jump right to the block section, but I encourage you to run through the step-by-step instructions presented first. Because the blocks are made one at a time, I chose simple techniques that were sufficient to make each block, based on how I saw components within the block. I think practicing these techniques is a great way to build your piecing skills.

Since there are no measurements included in the step-by-step instructions, use the cutting chart for each block you are making and cut pieces that pertain to the size of your block. The step-by-step technique will move you forward through the piecing process. If you are a beginner, these instructions are basic enough to get you started. If you are an experienced quilter, you can apply your shortcut skills wherever you have an opportunity.

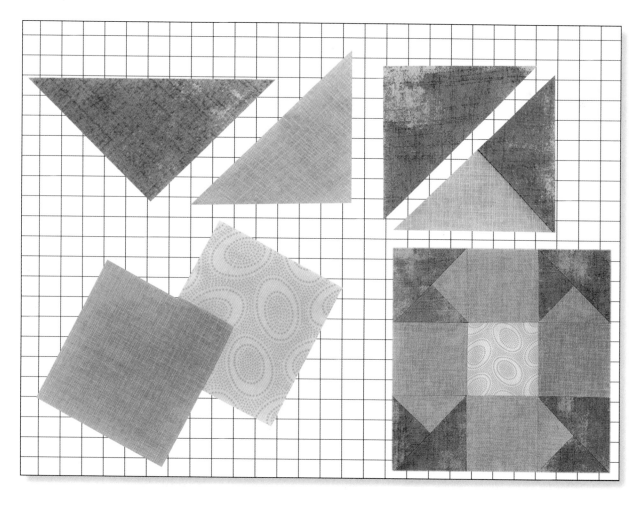

Half-Square Triangle Technique 1

Note: Once in a while, you will be cutting extra HST pieces, depending on the design of the blocks in this book. Set aside for another project.

Half-square triangles (HSTs) are used in a variety of block designs. The HST in this technique is made by cutting squares and then piecing two triangles together. To determine what size to cut fabric squares for HSTs, add ⅞" (2.22cm) to the finished size of the square.

1 Using the measurements from the cutting chart, cut each square in half diagonally from corner to corner using a ruler and rotary cutter. (You can draw the diagonal line in pencil first if you are not confident holding your ruler in place.)

2 Each square will yield two triangles.

3 Layer a light and dark triangle, RST (right sides together.) Sew a ¼" (0.64cm) seam along the long edge of the triangles.

4 Press the seam open. Trim fabric "tails."

Zig Zag Block

Use the instructions for Half-Square Triangle Technique 1 to practice making the Zig Zag Triangle Block. There are a total of 16 HSTs made individually.

Color / Cut		Subcut	6"	9"	12"
A White 8	☐	◺	2⅜"	3⅛"	3⅞"
B Floral 4	☐	◺	2⅜"	3⅛"	3⅞"
C Blue 4	☐	◺	2⅜"	3⅛"	3⅞"

Half-Square Triangle Technique 2

With the second HST technique you will sew seams before cutting the squares into triangles. This method is particularly useful when making several HSTs. The only difference between techniques 1 and 2 is the way the HST is constructed.

1 Using the measurements from the cutting chart, draw a diagonal line from corner to corner on the wrong side of the lighter square. Layer a light and dark square, RST.

2 Sew a ¼" (0.64cm) seam on either side of the drawn line. (You can either draw a sewing line, shown here as a dashed line, or use your ¼" (0.64cm) machine foot.)

3 Cut on the drawn line.

4 Press the seams open. Trim fabric "tails."

Star of the West Block

Use the instructions for Half-Square Triangle Technique 2 to practice making the Star of the West Block. Since it is made from only 2 colors, this is the perfect technique to make HSTs two at a time.

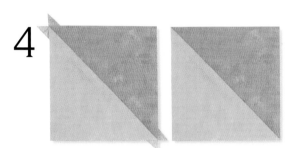

Color / Cut	Subcut	6"	9"	12"
A White 8		2⅜"	3⅛"	3⅞"
B Orange 8		2⅜"	3⅛"	3⅞"

Quarter-Square Triangle Technique 1

Note: Once in a while, you will be cutting extra QST pieces, depending on the design of the blocks in this book. Set aside for another project.

The Quarter-Square Triangle (QST) block is also referred to as an Hourglass block. To determine the cutting size, add 1¼" (3.18cm) to the finished size of the square for both QST techniques. Since you are sewing on the bias with this technique, handle gently to avoid stretching your pieces.

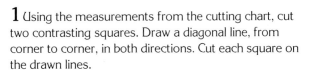

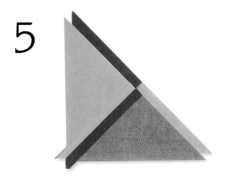

1 Using the measurements from the cutting chart, cut two contrasting squares. Draw a diagonal line, from corner to corner, in both directions. Cut each square on the drawn lines.

2 Each square will yield four triangles.

3 Lay out the block, alternating fabric as shown.

4 Layer a light and dark triangle, RST (right sides together.) Stitch with a ¼" (0.64cm) seam along a short edge of each pair of triangles. Press the seams toward the darker fabric.

5 Layer two pairs of triangles, RST with the light fabric on the dark, making sure seams are aligned. Sew a ¼" (0.64cm) seam along the long edge of the pair.

6 Press the seam and trim the fabric "tails."

Quarter-Square Triangle Technique 2

This technique is particularly useful when making several QSTs. This method can be interchanged with QST technique 1, depending on how many you need to make. Fabric is less likely to stretch since you are sewing on an uncut square.

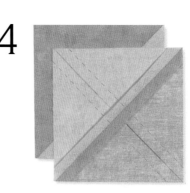

1 Using the measurements from the cutting chart, cut 2 squares of contrasting fabric. Draw a diagonal line from corner to corner on the wrong side of one block.

2 With RST, sew a ¼" (0.64cm) seam on either side of the drawn line. (You can either draw a sewing line, shown here as a dashed line, or use your ¼" (0.64cm) machine foot.)

3 Cut on the diagonal line to make two HSTs. Press seams open and trim fabric "tails."

4 Place the HSTs together with the light fabric on top of the dark fabric, matching diagonal seams. Draw a diagonal line from corner to corner on the wrong side of one HST.

5 Sew a ¼" (0.64cm) seam on either side of the drawn line. Cut on the diagonal line and press seams open. Trim fabric "tails."

6 This method will make two QSTs.

Flying Geese from Triangles

Whether you are making one or a few flying geese, this technique is the most basic to create a goose.

The large triangle is the "goose" body and the small triangles are the "sky." The body is cut from a quarter-square triangle. There may be left over pieces, depending on how many geese you make.

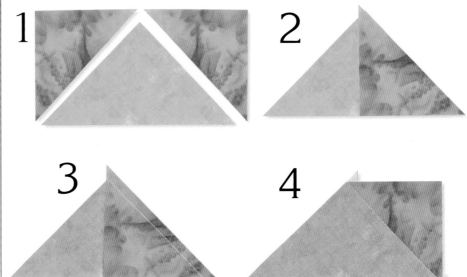

1 Use measurements from the cutting chart to create three triangles for a flying geese unit.

Note: The cutting chart will tell you to cut one square and subcut it diagonally twice from corner to corner. Depending on the block, you may have left over "body" triangles.

2 With RST (right sides together,) align the bottom and bias edge of a small "sky" triangle as shown. The corner of the "sky" should extend past the "goose."

3 Pin if you prefer, and sew along the long side of the "sky" triangle with a ¼" (0.64cm) seam.

4 Press seam away from "goose."

5 In the same manner, add the second small "sky" triangle to the opposite side of the "goose." Stitch along the long side of the sky triangle with a ¼" (0.64cm) seam.

6 Press seam away from "goose" and trim fabric "tails."

Flying Geese from Squares

In the second technique, squares are added to each corner of a rectangle to create a goose. Pieces to be used for Flying Geese from Squares are marked with an asterisk (*) in the cutting chart.

1 Using the measurements from the cutting chart, cut a rectangle and 2 squares for a flying geese unit. Draw a diagonal line from corner to corner on the wrong side of each of the smaller squares.

2 With RST, layer one square on a corner of the rectangle. Sew on the drawn line. Trim ¼" (0.64cm) from seam. Press seam toward smaller triangle.

3 With RST, layer the second square on the opposite corner, as shown. Sew on the drawn line. Trim corner ¼" (0.64cm) from seam. Press seam toward smaller triangle.

Good to Know

When you need to draw a sewing line, remember that the sewing line IS the edge of your ruler and it's impossible to draw a line at that point. Be sure to use a sharp-tipped pen or pencil and tip your marking tool at an angle, as shown, to get as close to the edge of your ruler as possible.

1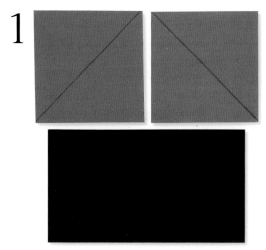

2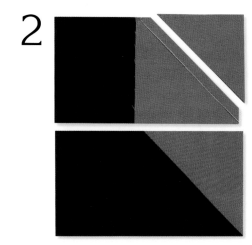

3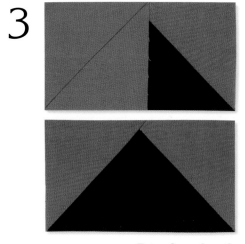

Four-at-a-Time Flying Geese

This no-waste method will yield four Flying Geese. This is the technique to use when there are four identical flying geese within a block. Pieces to be used for Four-at-a-Time Flying Geese are marked with an asterisk (*) in the cutting chart.

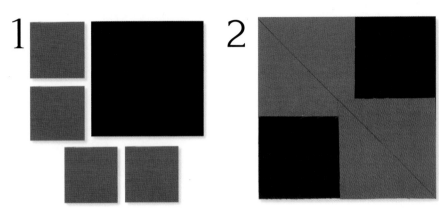

1 Using the measurements from the cutting chart, cut 1 large square for the "geese" and 4 small squares for the "sky" triangles.

2 Draw a diagonal line from corner to corner on the wrong side of all four of the small squares. With RST (right sides together,) layer and pin two squares on opposite corners of the large square as shown.

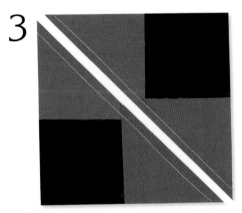

3 Sew a ¼" (0.64cm) seam on either side of the drawn line. Cut on drawn line to make two units.

4 Press smaller triangles away from the larger triangle on each of the units in step 3.

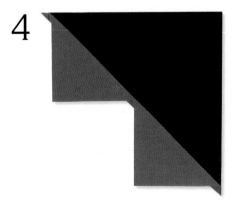

5 With RST, layer and pin one square on the corner of a unit from step 4.

6 Sew a ¼" (0.64cm) seam on either side of the drawn line. Cut on the drawn line. Press seams away from larger triangle. Repeat with second large triangle unit.

7 Press seams toward smaller triangles. Trim the fabric "tails."

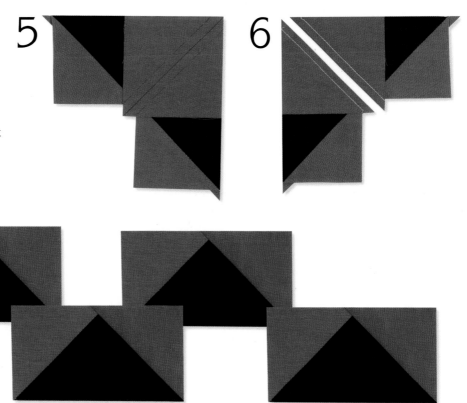

Spinning Geese Block

Use the Four-at-a-Time Flying Geese technique to practice making the Spinning Geese Block.

Color / Cut		Subcut	6"	9"	12"
A White 1	☐	◺	2⅜"	3⅛"	3⅞"
A White 4	☐	◺	4¼"	5¾"	7¼"
B Floral 1	☐	◺	4¼"	5¾"	7¼"
C Navy 4	☐	◺	2⅜"	3⅛"	3⅞"

Partial Seams

Partial seams are necessary when pieces "wrap" or "pinwheel" around a center square. There are only a couple of blocks in this book that use this technique but it's good to know how to sew these seams.

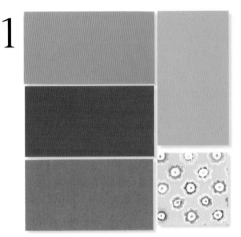

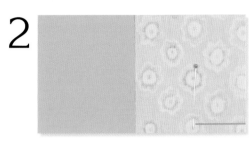

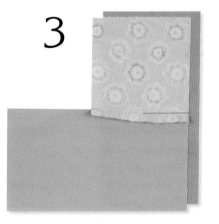

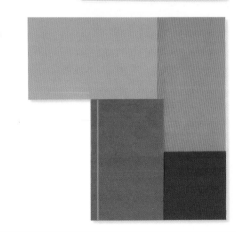

1 Using the measurements from the cutting chart, cut a square and four rectangles for the block.

2 With RST (right sides together,) sew the first rectangle to the center, beginning from the middle of the center square and locking your starting stitches. Finger press seam.

3 With RST, layer the partial seam unit from step 2 to the second rectangle, and sew ¼" (0.64cm) seam the length of the rectangle. Finger press the seam open.

4 With RST, sew the third rectangle onto the unit. Finger press the seam open.

5 Repeat step 4 with the final rectangle.

6 Turn block right side up. It will have a partially unsewn rectangle, as shown, ready to be sewn to complete the block.

7 Flip the unsewn rectangle down and align with the top of the center block, RST. Sew ¼" (0.64cm) partial seam to complete the block.

8 Press seams.

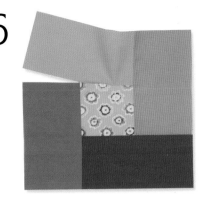

6

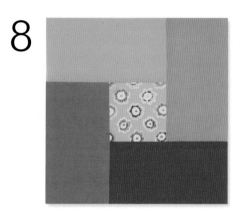

7

8

Good to Know

Fussy cutting is a way of isolating a favorite design or motif in a fabric and cutting out around it. If you want to replace a component in a block, cut it the same size, making sure there is a ¼" (0.64cm) on all sides of the design. This is a good time to use a large print as shown in this block.

Parallel Seams

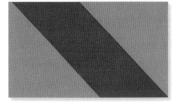

The parallel component is used in several quilt blocks, including the Magnolia block, page 144, and Pudding and Pie, page 147. It can also be used alone to make a zigzag or chevron quilt. Pieces to be used for a Parallel component are marked with an asterisk (*) in the cutting chart.

1

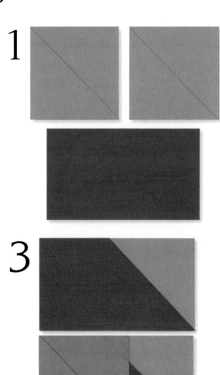

2

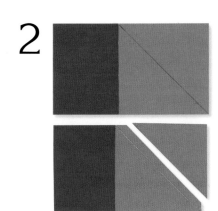

3

4

1 Using the measurements from the cutting chart, cut a rectangle and two squares. Draw a diagonal line from corner to corner on the wrong side of both small squares.

2 With RST (right sides together,) layer one square on top of the rectangle, as shown. Sew on drawn line. Trim ¼" (0.64cm) from sewn line.

3 Press seam open. Lay a small square on the opposite corner RST, with the drawn line parallel to first sewn line, as shown. Sew on drawn line. Trim ¼" (0.64cm) from seam.

4 Press seam open.

Note: See page 43 on how to use cutaway triangles.

Diamond Zig Zag Block

Use the Parallel Seams instructions to practice making the Diamond Zig Zag lock. Place 4 squares on rectangles with drawn lines facing left. Place the other 4 squares with sewn lines facing right. Parallel components should "mirror" one another to correctly make this block.

Color / Cut	6"	9"	12"
A Green 8 ▭	2" x 3½"	2¾" x 5"	3½" x 6½"
B Floral 16 ◻	2"	2¾"	3½"

Square-in-a-Square

This component is used in many block designs but can stand alone as a 2 x 2 (5.08 x 5.08 cm) grid block. The large center square can be fussy-cut for a different look.

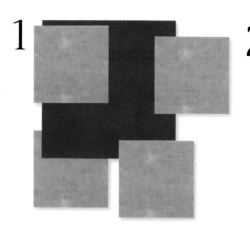

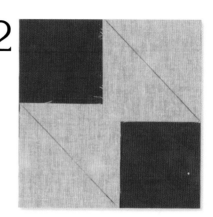

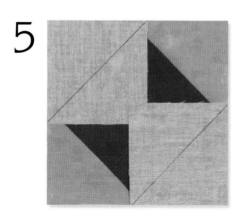

1 Using the measurements from the cutting chart, cut a large square and 4 small squares.

2 Draw a diagonal line from corner to corner on the wrong side of all 4 of the small squares. With RST, layer and pin two small squares on opposite corners as shown.

3 Sew on the drawn line. Trim corners ¼" (0.64cm) from seam.

Note: See page 43 on how to use cutaway triangles.

4 Press seams open.

5 Repeat with two additional squares on remaining corners as shown in step 3.

6 Trim ¼" (0.64cm) from seam and press seams open.

Note: This is a good block to check measurements after completed. Be sure it's square.

Adding Corners

These components are most often used to create more complex blocks, such as Flying Leaves, page 57 and Waypoint Star, page 110. Corners can be added to either squares or rectangles. Pieces to be used for these units are marked with an asterisk (*) in the cutting chart.

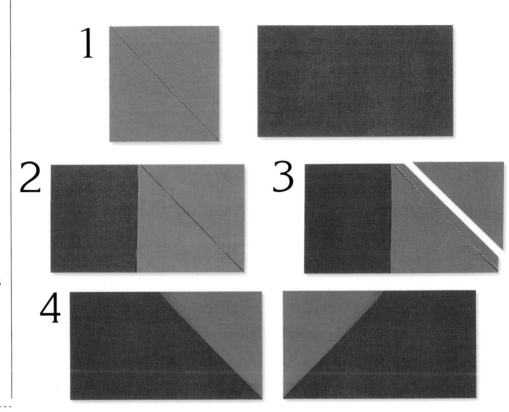

1 Using the measurements from the cutting chart, cut one rectangle and one square. Draw a diagonal line from corner to corner on the wrong side of the square.

2 To make a right corner block, align a small square RST (right sides together) along the right side of the rectangle, as shown.

3 Sew on the drawn line. Trim ¼" (0.64cm) from seam. Press seam open.

4 For a left corner block, repeat step 2 aligning the smaller square RST along the left side of the rectangle.

Adding Triangles to a Square

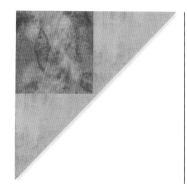

The half-square triangles in the block below change the look dramatically by piecing a square and two triangles of contrasting color or pattern.

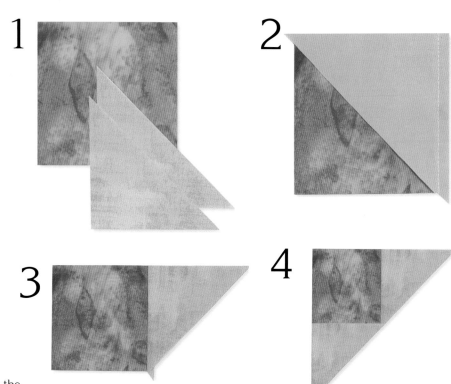

1 Cut a square and 2 triangles using the measurements in the cutting chart.

2 With RST, align the straight edge of the triangle to two sides of a square as shown. Sew on one short side using a ¼" (0.64cm) seam.

3 Press seam and trim the triangle "tail."

4 Repeat step 2 on the other side of the square, press the seam and trim the triangle "tail."

Triangles in a Row

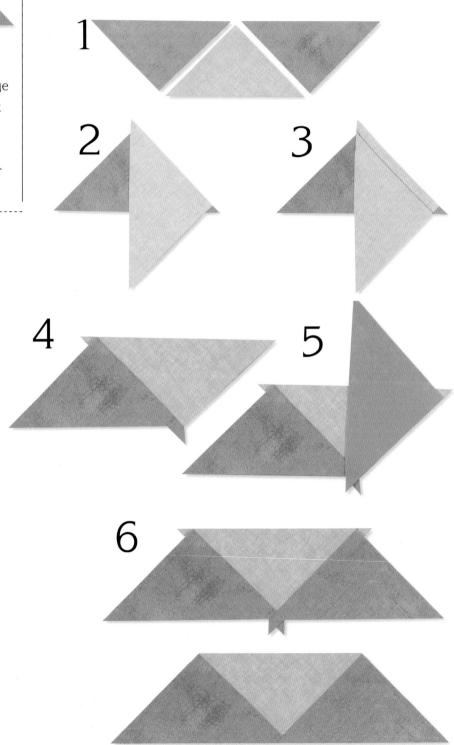

A few blocks require sewing triangles together in a row. (See North Wind block on page 66.) This technique is a must to guarantee the strip of triangles maintain their points when adding the other components of the block.

1 Lay out triangles as shown.

2 Layer a triangle, RST (right sides together) at a 90° angle, offsetting the top triangle ¼" (0.64cm) as shown.

3 Sew along the short side of the triangle set.

4 Press seam to one side.

5 Layer another triangle on top of set, offsetting a ¼" (0.64cm) as shown. Sew along the short side.

6 Press seam to one side. Trim the fabric "tails."

Making 3-Patch Half-Square Triangles

Three-patch half-square triangles are shown in "Dan's Mountain" (page 173). These blocks are made by using Quarter-Square Triangles Technique 1, on page 14. Follow steps 1–2 to cut pieces and orient the cuts to match the block. Sew the pieces together and add an HST to finish the block section. There will be times when you may have unused pieces. Set aside for another project.

Dan's Mountain" (page 173)

Good to Know

The more pieces in your block, the more pressing is necessary. I found that hanging my block over the edge of my ironing board made it easier to press seams without disturbing the ones I had already pressed.

The 2 x 2 Grid Blocks

A 2 x 2 grid block is a good starting point for beginners because the components are usually bigger. The process is the same; accurate cutting, accurate seams, gentle pressing. The block can be as simple as a four-patch in two colors. Start dissecting and the block will reveal pinwheels, big flying geese, contrasting half-square triangles, and arrows.

Big Dipper

QST—pages 14–15

Color/Cut	Subcut	4½"	6"	9"	12"
A 2 ☐	⊠	3½"	4¼"	5¾"	7¼"
B 1 ■	⊠	3½"	4¼"	5¾"	7¼"
C 1 ▨	⊠	3½"	4¼"	5¾"	7¼"

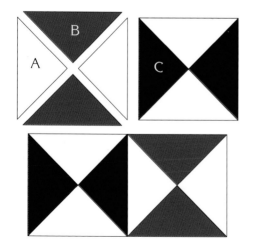

Broken Dishes

HST—pages 12–13

Color/Cut	Subcut	4½"	6"	9"	12"
A 2 ☐	◺	3⅛"	3⅞"	5⅜"	6⅞"
B 2 ■	◺	3⅛"	3⅞"	5⅜"	6⅞"

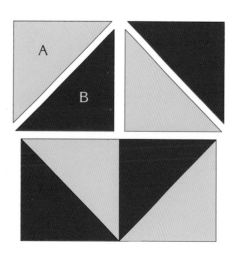

The 2 x 2 Grid Blocks

Buckeye Beauty

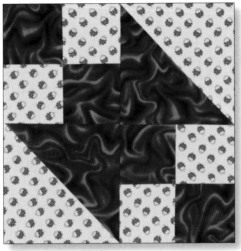

HST—pages 12–13

Color/Cut	Subcut	4½"	6"	9"	12"
A 4	☐	1⅝"	2"	2¾"	3½"
A 1	☐ ◺	2"	3⅞"	5⅜"	6⅞"
B 1	■ ◺	2"	3⅞"	5⅜"	6⅞"
B 4	■	1⅝"	2"	2¾"	3½"

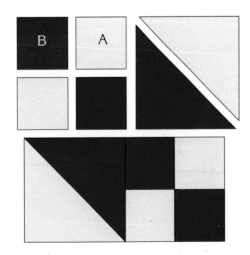

Carmen's Block

Color/Cut	Subcut	4½"	6"	9"	12"
A 2	☐	2¾	3½"	5"	6½"
B 4	▨	1⅝"	2"	2¾"	3½"
C 4	■	1⅝"	2"	2¾"	3½"

----TIPS----

A good block to practice matching seams.

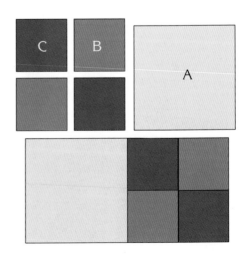

Caroline's Choice

HST—pages 12–13

Color/Cut	Subcut	4½"	6"	9"	12"
A 4		2	2⅜"	3⅛"	3⅞"
B 2		2¾"	3½"	5"	6½"
C 4		2	2⅜"	3⅛"	3⅞"

---TIPS---
HSTs make a simple pinwheel.

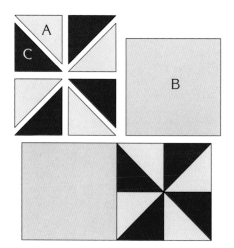

Cracker Block

HST—pages 12–13

Color/Cut	Subcut	4½"	6"	9"	12"
A 1		3⅛"	3⅞"	5⅜"	6⅞"
A 1		1⅝" x 3⅝"	2" x 4¾"	2⅝" x 6⅞"	3⅜" x 9"
B 1		3⅛"	3⅞"	5⅜"	6⅞"
B 2		1½" x 3⅝"	3⅝" x 4¾"	2⅝" x 6⅞"	3⅜" x 9"

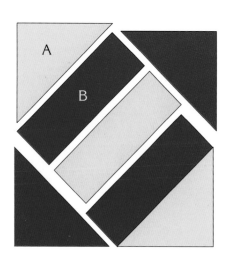

Crosses and Losses

HST—pages 12–13

Color/Cut	Subcut	4½"	6"	9"	12"
A 1	⬜ ◺	3⅛"	3⅞"	5⅜"	6⅞"
A 4	⬜	1⅝"	2"	2¾"	3½"
A 2	⬜ ◹	2"	2⅜"	3⅛"	3⅞"
B 1	⬛ ◺	3⅛"	3⅞"	5⅜"	6⅞"
B 2	⬛ ◺	2"	2⅜"	3⅛"	3⅞"

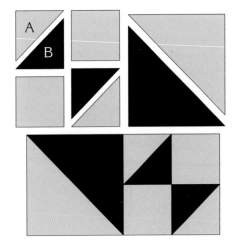

Double Pinwheel

HST—pages 12–13
QST—page 14 (steps 1–4)

Color/Cut	Subcut	4½"	6"	9"	12"
A 2	⬜ ◺	3⅛"	3⅞"	5⅜"	6⅞"
B 1	⬜ ⊠	3½"	4¼"	5¾"	7¼"
C 1	⬛ ⊠	3½"	4¼"	5¾"	7¼"

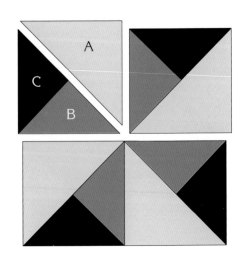

Double X Block #1

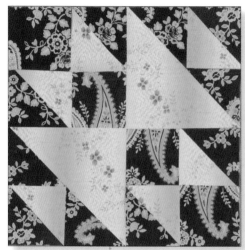

HST—pages 12–13
Adding Triangles to a Square—page 25

Color/Cut	Subcut		4½"	6"	9"	12"
A 1	⬜	◺	3⅛"	3⅞"	5⅜"	6⅞"
A 3	⬜	◺ 2	2⅜"	3⅛"	3⅞"	
B 4	⬛		1⅝"	2"	2¾"	3½"
B 5	⬛	◺ 2	2⅜"	3⅛"	3⅞"	

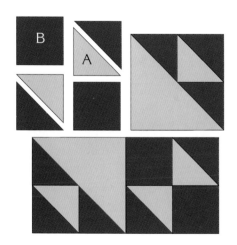

Flock of Geese

HST—pages 12–13

Color/Cut	Subcut		4½"	6"	9"	12"
A 1	⬜	◺	3⅛"	3⅞"	5⅜"	6⅞"
A 2	⬜	◺ 2	2⅜"	3⅛"	3⅞"	
B 1	⬛	◺	3⅛"	3⅞"	5⅜"	6⅞"
B 2	⬛		2	2⅜"	3⅜"	3⅞"

---TIPS---
Check sizes of your HST's for accuracy
before putting this block together.

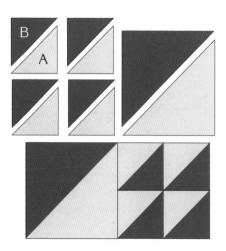

Flying Dutchman

Flying Geese from Squares—page 17
QST—page 14

Color/Cut	Subcut	4½"	6"	9"	12"
A 2	⊠	2"	3¼"	4¼"	5¼
*A 8		1¼"	1½"	2"	2½"
B 2	⊠	2"	3¼"	4¼"	5¼"
*B 4		1¼" x 2"	1½" x 2½"	2" x 3½"	2½" x 4½"
B 4		1¼" x 2¾"	1½" x 3½"	2" x 5"	2½" x 6½"

┄ TIPS ┄
*Use 8 squares and 4 rectangles to make
Flying Geese from Squares on page 17.

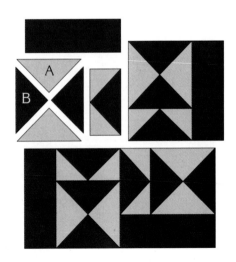

Forward and Back

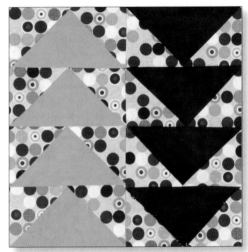

Flying Geese from Squares—page 17

Color/Cut	Subcut	4½"	6"	9"	12"
A 4		1⅝" x 2¾"	2" x 3½"	2¾" x 5"	3½" x 6½"
B 16		1⅝"	2"	2¾"	3½"
C 4		1⅝" x 2¾"	2" x 3½"	2¾" x 5"	3½" x 6½"

┄ TIPS ┄
Note: Use the squares and rectangles to make
Flying Geese from Squares on page 17.

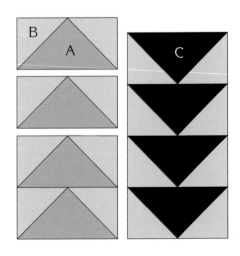

Four Patch Variation

Color/Cut	Subcut		4½"	6"	9"	12"
A 2			1⅝"	2"	2¾"	3½"
B 2			1⅝"	2"	2¾"	3½"
B 2			1⅝" x 2¾"	2" x 3½"	2¾" x 5"	3½" x 6½"
C 2			2¾"	3½"	5"	6½"

----- TIPS -----
This is a simple block for a beginner.
Make it in three sizes for practice.

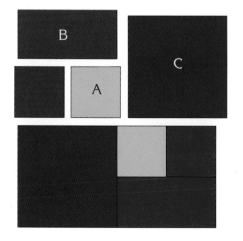

Goday Design

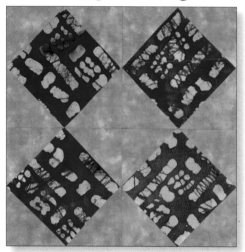

Square-in-a-Square—page 23

Color/Cut	Subcut		4½"	6"	9"	12"
A 16			1⅝"	2"	2¾"	3½"
B 4			2¾"	3½"	5"	6½"

----- TIPS -----
Check measurements of the square-in-a-square; it
should be square! Trim if necessary.

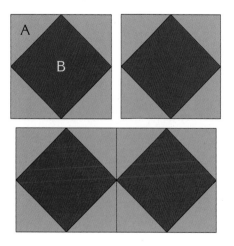

Hidden Square

Adding Triangles to a Square—page 25

Color/Cut	Subcut			4½"	6"	9"	12"
A 1	▨		◺	3⅛"	3⅞"	5⅜"	6⅞"
B 1	■			2¾"	3½"	5"	6½"
B 1	■		◺	5¾"	6⅞"	9⅞"	12⅞"

--- TIPS ---
There will be a triangle left over from HST B subcut.

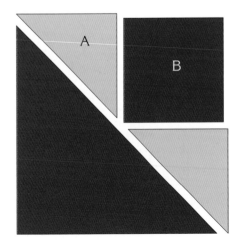

Homeward Bound

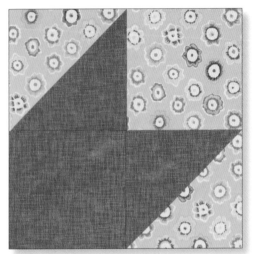

HST—pages 12–13

Color/Cut	Subcut		4½"	6"	9"	12"
A 1	▨		2¾"	3½"	5"	6½"
A 1	▨	◹	3⅛"	3⅞"	5⅜"	6⅞"
B 1	■	◹	3⅛"	3⅞"	5⅜"	6⅞"
B 1	■		2¾"	3½"	5"	6½"

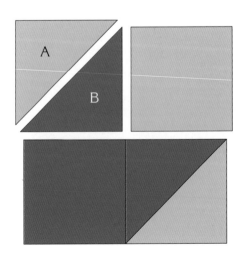

Linoleum Patch

Color/Cut	Subcut	4½"	6"	9"	12"
A 2		1⅝" x 2¾"	1½" x 3½"	2" x 5"	2½" x 6½"
B 2		2¾"	3½"	5"	6½"
C 4		1⅝" x 2¾"	1½" x 3½"	2" x 5"	2½" x 6½"

```
┌──────── TIPS ────────┐
Check your ¼" seams when sewing A & C.
Make sure the 3-strip unit is square.
└──────────────────────┘
```

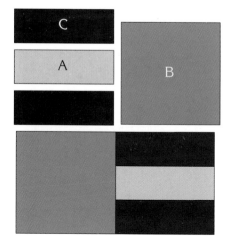

Louisiana Pinwheel

Flying Geese from Squares—page 17

Color/Cut	Subcut	4½"	6"	9"	12"
A 4		1⅝" x 2¾"	2" x 3½"	2¾" x 5"	3½" x 6½"
*B 8		1⅝"	2"	2¾"	3½"
*C 4		1⅝" x 2¾"	2" x 3½"	2¾" x 5"	3½" x 6½"

```
┌──────── TIPS ────────┐
*Use B squares and C rectangles to
make Flying Geese from Squares on page 17.
└──────────────────────┘
```

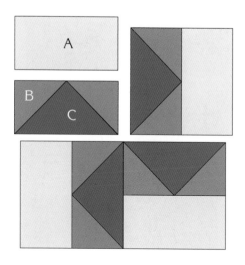

The 2 x 2 Grid Blocks

Railroad Crossing

HST—pages 12–13

Color/Cut	Subcut	4½"	6"	9"	12"
A 1	▫ ◨	2	3⅞"	5⅜"	6⅞"
A 4	▫	1⅝"	2"	2¾"	3½"
B 4	◼	1⅝"	2"	2¾"	3½"
C 1	◼ ◹	3⅛"	3⅞"	5⅜"	6⅞"

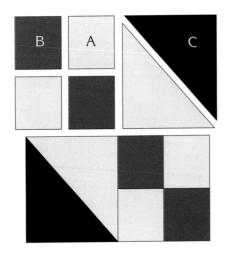

Right and Left

QST—pages 14 (steps 1–4)

Color/Cut	Subcut	4½"	6"	9"	12"
A 1	◼	5	6½"	9½"	12½"
A 2	◼ ⊠	3½"	4¼"	5¾"	7¼"
B 2	◼ ⊠	3⅛"	4¼"	5¾"	7¼"

-TIPS-
Mark the center on each edge of the square.
It helps center the triangle sets.

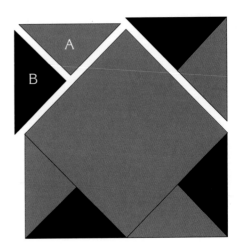

Slanted Diamonds

Parallel Seams—page 22

Color/Cut	Subcut	4½"	6"	9"	12"
A 4		2¾"	3½"	5"	6½"
B 2		2¾" x 5	3½" x 6½"	5" x 9½"	6½" x 12½"

----- TIPS -----
Note: Use the squares and rectangles
to make parallel seams on page 22.

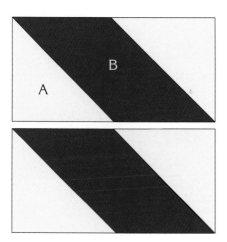

Southern Belle

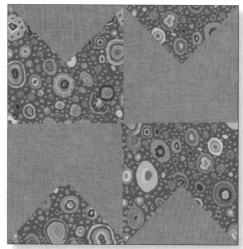

HST—pages 12–13
QST—page 14 (steps 1–4)

Color/Cut	Subcut	4½"	6"	9"	12"
A 1		3⅛"	3⅞"	5⅜"	6⅞"
A 1		3½"	4¼"	5¾"	7¼"
B 1		3⅛"	3⅞"	5⅜"	6⅞"
B 1		3½"	4¼"	5¾"	7¼"

----- TIPS -----
The square component with three triangles is sometimes
referred to as a "three patch quarter-square triangle."

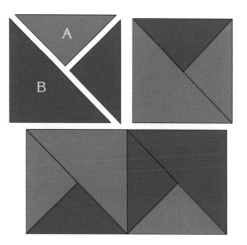

The 2 x 2 Grid Blocks

Spin City

HST—pages 12–13
Adding Triangles to a Square—page 25

Color/Cut		Subcut	4½"	6"	9"	12"
A 2			3⅛"	3⅞"	5⅜"	6⅞"
B 4			1⅝"	2"	2¾"	3½"
C 4			2"	2⅜"	3⅛"	3⅞"

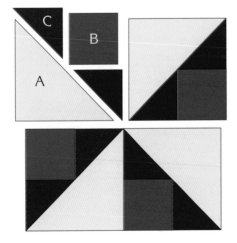

The Sickle

HST—pages 12–13

Color/Cut		Subcut	4½"	6"	9"	12"
A 4			1⅝"	2"	2¾"	3½"
A 1			3⅛"	3⅞"	5⅜"	6⅞"
B 4			1⅝"	2"	2¾"	3½"
C 1			3⅛"	3⅞"	5⅜"	6⅞"

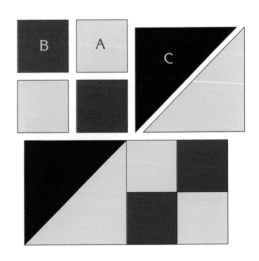

Turnstile Block

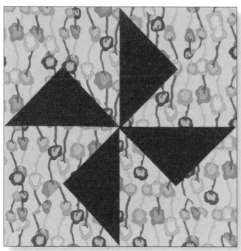

HST—pages 12–13
QST—page 14 (steps 1–4)

Color/Cut			Subcut	4½"	6"	9"	12"
A 2			2	3⅞"	5⅜"	6⅞"
A 1				2⅜"	4¼"	5¾"	7¼"
B 1				2⅜"	4¼"	5¾"	7¼"

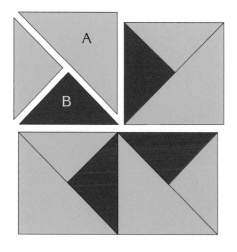

Two by Two

Color/Cut		Subcut	4½"	6"	9"	12"
A 4			1⅝" x 2¾"	2" x 3½"	2¾" x 5"	3½" x 6½"
B 2			1⅝" x 2¾"	2" x 3½"	2¾" x 5"	3½" x 6½"
C 2			1⅝" x 2¾"	2" x 3½"	2¾" x 5"	3½" x 6½"

---TIPS---
Another easy block using a rectangle shape.

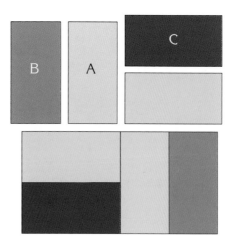

Wild Geese Fancy Flight

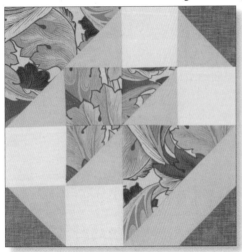

HST—pages 12–13; Adding Corners—page 24;
Adding Triangles to a Square—page 25

Color/Cut	Subcut		4½"	6"	9"	12"
A 4	▢		1⅝"	2"	2¾"	3½"
B 1	▢	◺	3⅛"	3⅞"	5⅜"	6⅞"
B 3	▢	◺	2"	2⅜"	3⅛"	3⅞"
C 1	▢	◺	2"	2⅜"	3⅛"	3⅞"
*C 1	▢		1⅝"	2"	2¾"	3½"
D 1	▢	◺	2"	2⅜"	3⅛"	3⅞"
D 1	▢		1⅝"	2"	2¾"	3½"
D 1	▢	◺	3⅛"	4¼"	5¾"	7¼"

TIPS
There will be a left over B HST.
*For Adding Corners, page 24, use C square.

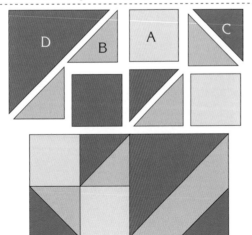

Wild Goose Chase

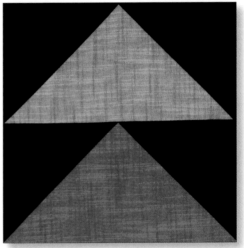

Flying Geese from Squares—page 17

Color/Cut	Subcut	4½"	6"	9"	12"
*A 1	▭	2¾" x 5	3½" x 6½"	5 x 9½"	6½" x 12½"
*B 1	▭	2¾" x 5	3½" x 6½"	5 x 9½"	6½" x 12½"
*C 4	◼	2¾"	3½"	5"	6½"

TIPS
*Use the squares and rectangles to make Flying Geese from Squares on page 17.

Note: This block can be made from 4-HSTs. But this technique alleviates a seam running through the "goose."

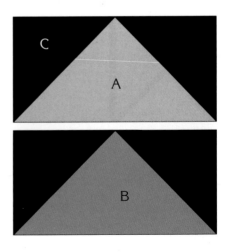

Good to Know

Chain piecing is a time and thread-saver even in a single block. Anytime there are multiple pieces in a block, like these HSTs, give this technique a try.

1 Layer triangles, RST, as shown. Place a leader (page 9) under presser foot, sew off the edge, leaving thread, and follow with the first triangle set.

2 Without cutting the thread, continue adding triangle sets. You will have a long chain of pieces.

3 Snip threads that attach pieces. Press.

Good to Know

"Waste Triangles" are those corner pieces that are cut off when you use squares to make Flying Geese, parallel blocks, or other components. Here is a quick way to mark, sew and cut off corners and have the waste triangle ready to press and use in another project.

1 When you need to draw a sewing line corner to corner, draw an additional line ½" parallel to it. Sew on both lines.

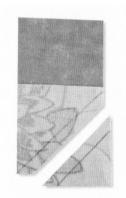

2 Cut between the lines creating two ¼" seam allowances.

3 Press seams. Depending on the component you are making, you may have multiple HSTs. Each Flying Geese unit yields two leftover HSTs.

The 3 x 3 Grid Blocks

Detail starts to surface in 3 x 3 grid blocks because there are nine identical squares that can be divided and sub-divided. An hour glass, flying geese, and spinning pinwheels appear as you increase the sub-division and complexity of the block. 3 x 3 grid blocks sit very well next to 6 x 6 grid blocks of the same size in a quilt setting. The seams align to give an even appearance.

A Dandy Quilt Block

HST—pages 12–13
Adding Corners—page 24

Color/Cut	Subcut		4½"	6"	9"	12"
*A 8			1¼"	1½"	2"	2½"
B 2		◺	2⅜"	2⅞"	3⅞"	4⅞"
C 1			2	2½"	3½"	4½"
C 2		◺	2⅜"	2⅞"	3⅞"	4⅞"
*D 4			2	2½"	3½"	4½"

TIPS
*For Adding Corners, page 24,
use A squares and D squares.

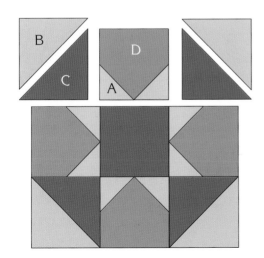

Air Castle

HST—pages 12–13; QST—page 14 (steps 1–4)
Square-in-a-Square—page 23

Color/Cut	Subcut		4½"	6"	9"	12"
A 2		◺	2⅜"	2⅞"	3⅞"	4⅞"
A 1		⊠	2¾"	3¼"	4¼"	5¼"
B 1		⊠	2¾"	3¼"	4¼"	5¼"
B 2		◺	2⅜"	2⅞"	3⅞"	4⅞"
C 2		◺	2⅜"	2⅞"	3⅞"	4⅞"
C 4			1¼"	1½"	2"	2½"
D 1			2"	2½"	3½"	4½"

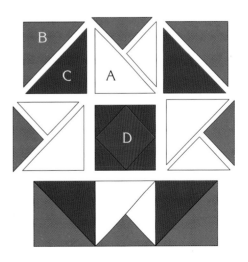

Album Star

Flying Geese from Triangles—page 16

Color/Cut	Subcut		4½"	6"	9"	12"
A 4			1⅝"	2"	2¾"	3½"
A 1	⊠		3½"	4¼"	5¾"	7¼"
A 1			1⅝" x 2¾"	1½" x 3½"	2" x 5"	2½" x 6½"
B 4	◹		2	2⅜"	3⅛"	3⅞"
B 2			1⅝" x 2¾"	1½'" x 3½"	2" x 5"	2½" x 6½"

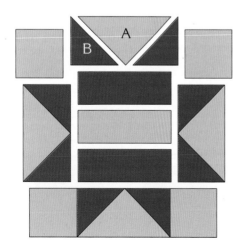

Antique Tiles

Color/Cut	Subcut		4½"	6"	9"	12"
A 4			1¼" x 2"	1½" x 2½"	2" x 3½"	2½" x 4½"
B 4			1¼" x 2"	1½" x 2½"	2" x 3½"	2½" x 4½"
B 4			1¼"	1½"	2"	2½"
C 1			2	2½"	3½"	4½"
C 4			1¼" x 2"	1½" x 2½"	2" x 3½"	2½" x 4½"
C 4			2	1½"	2"	2½"

-----TIPS-----
Lots of seams to match in this block!
It will help to use pins when piecing this block.

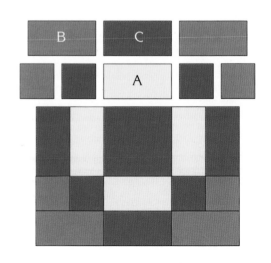

Art Square

Flying Geese from Squares—page 17

Color/Cut	Subcut	4½"	6"	9"	12"
A 4		1⅝"	2"	2¾"	3½"
B 1		2¾"	3½"	5"	6½"
*B 4		1⅝" x 2¾"	2" x 3½"	2¾" x 5"	3½" x 6½"
*C 8		1⅝"	2"	2¾"	3½"

─── TIPS ───
*Use C squares and B rectangles to make
Flying Geese from Squares, page 17.

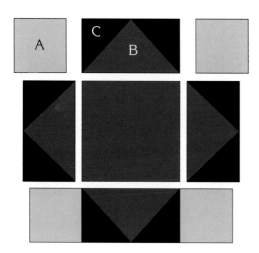

Aunt Malvernia

QST—pages 14–15

Color/Cut	Subcut	4½"	6"	9"	12"
A 5	⊠	2¾"	3¼"	4¼"	5¼"
B 5	⊠	2¾"	3¼"	4¼"	5¼"

─── TIPS ───
There will be triangles left over from A and B QST subcuts.
Pay attention to orientation of QSTs.

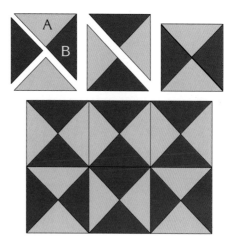

Balkan Variation

HST—pages 12–13; Square-in-a-Square—page 23
Flying Geese from Squares—page 17

Color/Cut	Subcut	4½"	6"	9"	12"
A 1	☐	2¾"	3½"	5"	6½"
A 4	☐	1⅝"	2	2¾"	3½"
A 2	☐◹	2"	2⅜"	3⅛"	3⅞"
*B 4	◼	1⅝"	2	2¾"	3½"
B 2	◼◹	2	2⅜"	3⅛"	3⅞"
C 4	◼	1⅝"	2	2¾"	3½"
*C 4	▬	1⅝" x 2¾"	2" x 3½"	2¾" x 5"	3½" x 6½"

TIPS

*Use A and B squares, and C rectangles to make
Flying Geese from Squares, page 17.

Each goose has "light and dark" sky colors.

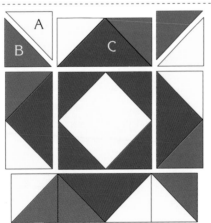

Bell's Favorite

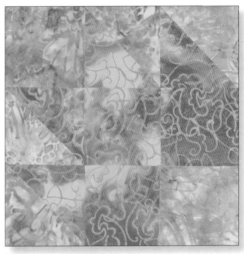

HST—pages 12–13

Color/Cut	Subcut	4½"	6"	9"	12"
A 2	◼	2"	2½"	3½"	4½"
A 2	◼◹	2⅜"	2⅞"	3⅞"	4⅞"
B 2	◼◹	2⅜"	2⅞"	3⅞"	4⅞"
B 3	◼	2"	2½"	3½"	4½"

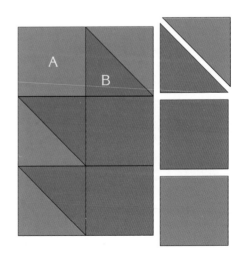

Bear Tracks

Square-in-a-Square—page 23

Color/Cut		Subcut	4½"	6"	9"	12"
A 2			1⅝" x 2¾"	2" x 3½"	2¾" x 5"	3½" x 6½"
A 8			1⅝"	2"	2¾"	3½"
B 4			1⅝"	2"	2¾"	3½"
B 2			2¾"	3½"	5"	6½"

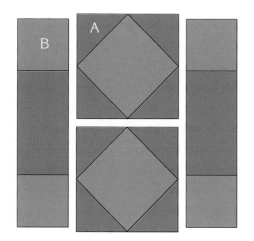

Big O Block

HST—pages 12–13

Color/Cut		Subcut	4½"	6"	9"	12"
A 1			2"	2½"	3½"	4½"
A 2		◹	2⅜"	2⅞"	3⅞"	4⅞"
B 2		◹	2⅜"	2⅞"	3⅞"	4⅞"
B 4			2"	2½"	3½"	4½"

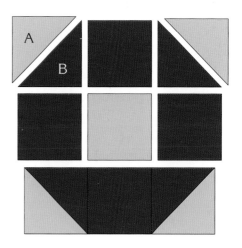

The 3 x 3 Grid Blocks

Big T Block

HST—pages 12–13
Flying Geese from Triangles—page 16

Color/Cut		Subcut	4½"	6"	9"	12"
A 2		◻	2⅜"	2⅞"	3⅞"	4⅞"
*A 1		⊠	2¾"	3¼"	4¼"	5¼"
B 4			1¼" x 2"	1½" x 2½"	2" x 3½"	2½" x 4½"
*C 4		◻	1⅝"	1⅞"	2⅜"	2⅞"
D 1			2"	2½"	3½"	4½"
D 2		◻	2⅜"	2⅞"	3⅞"	4⅞"

------ TIPS ------
*Use the QST A pieces for "body" of flying geese
and HST C pieces for "sky" to make
Flying Geese from Triangles, page 16.

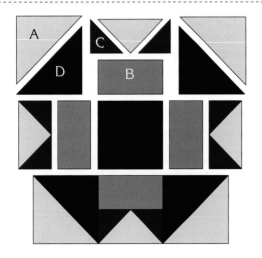

Birds In The Air

HST—pages 12–13
Adding Triangles to a Square—page 25.

Color/Cut		Subcut	4½"	6"	9"	12"
A 1		◻	5⅜"	6⅞"	9⅞"	12⅞"
A 2		◻	2⅜"	2⅞"	3⅞"	4⅞"
B 3		◻	2⅜"	2⅞"	3⅞"	4⅞"

------ TIPS ------
There will be triangles left over from both A HST subcuts.

Make the large pieced triangle then sew to "A"
triangle on the diagonal.

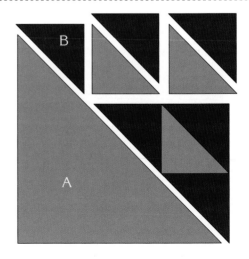

Birds In The Air Variation

HST—pages 12–13

Color/Cut	Subcut		4½"	6"	9"	12"
A 1			3½"	4½"	6½"	8½"
A 3		◹	2⅜"	2⅞"	3⅞"	4⅞"
B 3		◹	2⅜"	2⅞"	3⅞"	4⅞"

--- TIPS ---
There will be triangles left over from A & B HST subcuts.

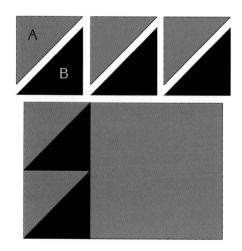

Blades Block

HST—pages 12–13

Color/Cut	Subcut		4½"	6"	9"	12"
A 2		◹	2⅜"	2⅞"	3⅞"	4⅞"
B 1			2"	2½"	3½"	4½"
C 4			1¼"	1½"	2'	2½"
D 2		◹	2⅜"	2⅞"	3⅞"	4⅞"
D 4			1¼"	1½"	2'	2½"
D 4			1¼" x 2"	1½" x 2½"	2" x 3½"	2½" x 4½"

--- TIPS ---
Pay attention to the orientation of the 4 corner HSTs.

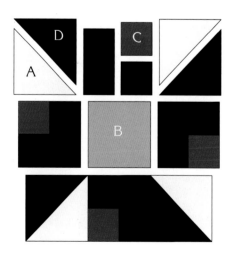

Blocks In A Row

Color/Cut	Subcut	4½"	6"	9"	12"
A 1		2"	2½"	3½"	4½"
B 2		2"	2½"	3½"	4½"
B 2		2" x 5½"	2½" x 6½"	3½" x 9½"	4½" x 12½"

─── TIPS ───
You can "fussy cut" the A block as shown,
or use a contrasting solid.

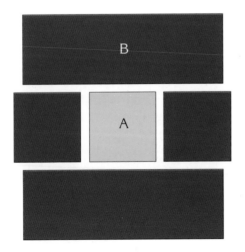

Bright Hopes

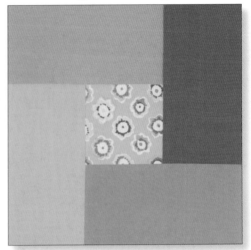

Partial Seams—page 20

Color/Cut	Subcut	4½"	6"	9"	12"
A 1		2"	2½"	3½"	4½"
B 1		2 x 3½"	2½" x 4½"	3½" x 6½"	4½" x 8½"
C 1		2 x 3½"	2½" x 4½"	3½" x 6½"	4½" x 8½"
D 1		2 x 3½"	2½" x 4½"	3½" x 6½"	4½" x 8½"
E 1		2 x 3½"	2½" x 4½"	3½" x 6½"	4½" x 8½"

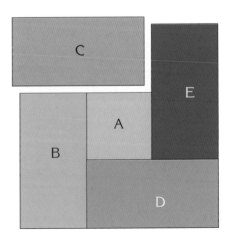

Calico Puzzle

HST—pages 12–13

Color/Cut	Subcut		4½"	6"	9"	12"
A 2	☐	◱	2⅜"	2⅞"	3⅞"	4⅞"
B 2	◩	◱	2⅜"	2⅞"	3⅞"	4⅞"
B 1	◪		2"	2½"	3½"	4½"
C 4	■		2"	2½"	3½"	4½"

----- TIPS -----
Pay attention to the orientation of the corner HSTs.

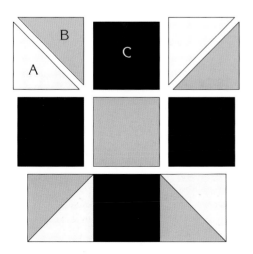

Card Trick

HST—pages 12–13; QST—page 14 (steps 1–4)

Color/Cut	Subcut		4½"	6"	9"	12"
A 2	☐	◳	2⅜"	2⅞"	3⅞"	4⅞"
A 1	☐	⊠	2¾"	3¼"	4¼"	5¼"
B 1	■	◱	2⅜"	2⅞"	3⅞"	4⅞"
B 1	■	⊠	2¾"	3¼"	4¼"	5¼"
C 1	■	◳	2⅜"	2⅞"	3⅞"	4⅞"
C 1	■	⊠	2¾"	3¼"	4¼"	5¼"
D 1	■	◱	2⅜"	2⅞"	3⅞"	4⅞"
D 1	■	⊠	2¾"	3¼"	4¼"	5¼"
E 1	■	◳	2⅜"	2⅞"	3⅞"	4⅞"
E 1	■	⊠	2¾"	3¼"	4¼"	5¼"

----- TIPS -----
You will have triangles left from B, C, D, & E QST subcuts.

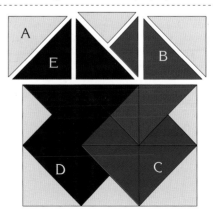

Celestial Block

HST—pages 12–13
Flying Geese from Triangles—page 16

Color/Cut		Subcut	4½"	6"	9"	12"
A 4			1⅝"	2"	2¾"	3½"
B 1		◩	2"	2⅜"	3⅛"	3⅞"
C 1		◩	3⅛"	3⅞"	5⅜"	6⅞"
D 1		◩	2"	2⅞"	3⅛"	3⅞"
E 1		◩	3⅛"	3⅞"	5⅜"	6⅞"
F 2			1⅝"	2"	2¾"	3½"
F 2		◩	2"	2⅜"	3⅛"	3⅞"
F 2			1⅝" x 2¾"	2" x 3½"	2¾" x 5"	3½" x 6½"

---TIPS---
There will be triangles left over from C & E HST subcuts.

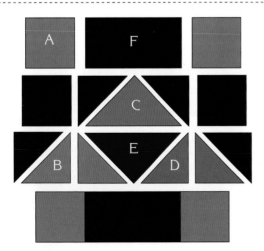

Churn Dash

HST—pages 12–13

Color/Cut		Subcut	4½"	6"	9"	12"
A 4			1¼" x 2"	1½" x 2½"	2" x 3½"	2½" x 4½"
B 1			2"	2½"	3½"	4½"
B 2		◩	2⅜"	2⅞"	3⅞"	4⅞"
C 4			1¼" x 2"	1½" x 2½"	2" x 3½"	2½" x 4½"
C 2		◩	2⅜"	2⅞"	3⅞"	4⅞"

---TIPS---
Measure each of the nine units before
constructing block. Units should be square.

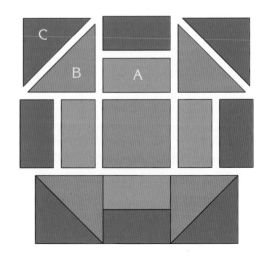

Combination Star

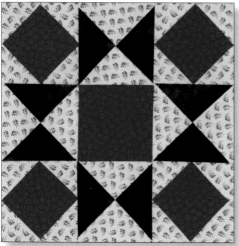

QST—page 15
Square-in-a-Square—page 23

Color/Cut		Subcut	4½"	6"	9"	12"
A 16			1¼"	1½"	2"	2½"
A 2		⊠	2¾"	3¼"	4¼"	5¼"
B 5			2"	2½"	3½"	4½"
C 2		⊠	2¾"	3¼"	4¼"	5¼"

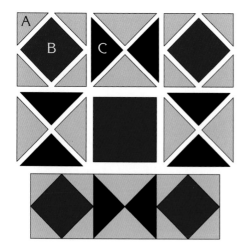

Double Monkey Wrench

Color/Cut		Subcut	4½"	6"	9"	12"
A 1			2"	2½"	3½"	4½"
A 2		◺	2⅜"	2⅞"	3⅞"	4⅞"
B 4			1¼" x 2	1½" x 2½"	2" x 3½"	2½" x 4½"
C 4			1¼" x 2	1½" x 2½"	2" x 3½"	2½" x 4½"
C 2		◺	2⅜"	2⅞"	3⅞"	4⅞"

────TIPS────
Experiment with this block
by switching lights and darks.

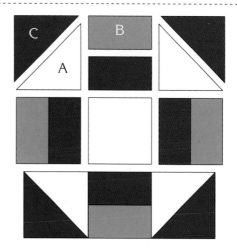

Double Necktie

Adding Corners—page 24

Color/Cut	Subcut	4½"	6"	9"	12"
A 4		2"	2½"	3½"	4½"
*A 4		1¼"	1½"	2"	2½"
*B 5		2"	2½"	3½"	4½"

┌─── TIPS ───┐
*For Adding Corners, page 24,
use 4-A squares and 3-B squares.
└────────────┘

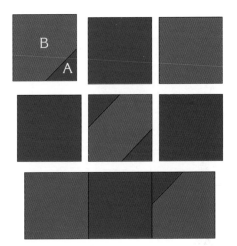

Double X Block #2

HST—pages 12–13

Color/Cut	Subcut		4½"	6"	9"	12"
A 2		◺	2⅜"	2⅞"	3⅞"	4⅞"
B 1			2"	2½"	3½"	4½"
C 1		◺	2⅜"	2⅞"	3⅞"	4⅞"
D 2		◺	2"	2½"	3½"	4½"
D 3			2⅜"	2⅞"	3⅞"	4⅞"

┌─── TIPS ───┐
This is a good block to lay out all of the pieces
correctly, then sew in rows.
└────────────┘

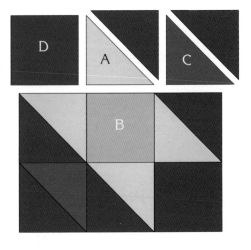

Eccentric Star

HST—pages 12–13

Color/Cut	Subcut	4½"	6"	9"	12"
A 4		2⅜"	2⅞"	3⅞"	4⅞"
B 2		2⅜"	2⅞"	3⅞"	4⅞"
B 1		2"	2½"	3½"	4½"
C 2		2⅜"	2⅞"	3⅞"	4⅞"

---TIPS---
Pay attention to the orientation of HSTs in this block.

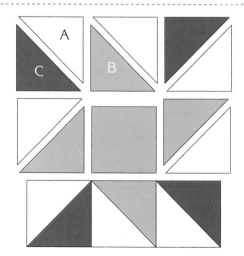

Flying Leaves

Adding Corners—page 24

Color/Cut	Subcut	4½"	6"	9"	12"
*A 9		2"	2½"	3½"	4½"
*B 10		1¼"	1½"	2"	2½"

---TIPS---
For Adding Squares, page 24,
use 6-A squares and 10-B squares.

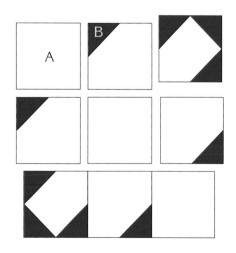

Four Square

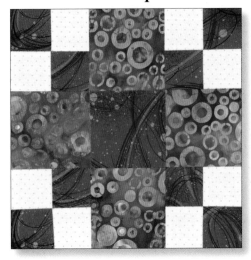

Color/Cut	Subcut	4½"	6"	9"	12"
A 8	⬜	1¼"	1½"	2"	2½"
B 8	⬛	1¼"	1½"	2"	2½"
B 1	⬛	2"	2½"	3½"	4½"
C 4	▨	2"	2½"	3½"	4½"

TIPS
Make sure pieced squares are
square in this 3 x 3 grid.

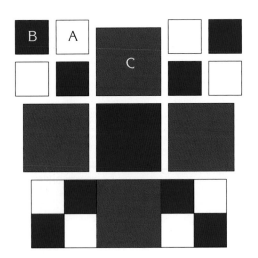

Four Square Variation

Color/Cut	Subcut	4½"	6"	9"	12"
A 8	⬜	1¼"	1½"	2"	2½"
A 4	⬜	2"	2½"	3½"	4½"
B 8	⬛	1¼"	1½"	2"	2½"
B 1	⬛	2"	2½"	3½"	4½"

TIPS
This variation of the Four Square Block
is nothing more than a color change.

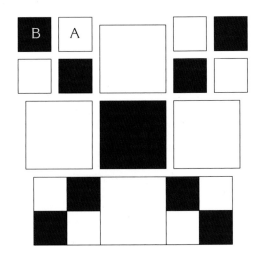

Gallery Star

QST—page 14

Color/Cut	Subcut	4½"	6"	9"	12"
A 5		2"	2½"	3½"	4½"
A 1	⊠	2¾"	3¼"	4¼"	5¼"
B 1	⊠	2¾"	3¼"	4¼"	5¼"
C 1	⊠	2¾"	3¼"	4¼"	5¼"
D 1	⊠	2¾"	3¼"	4¼"	5¼"

─────── TIPS ───────
Pay attention to color orientation in QSTs.

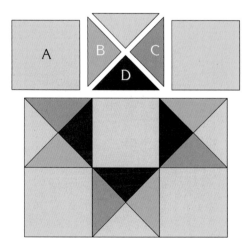

Green River

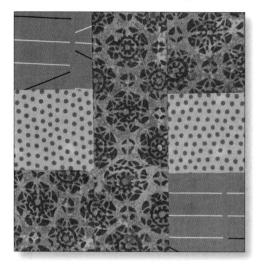

Color/Cut	Subcut	4½"	6"	9"	12"
A 2		2"	2½"	3½"	4½"
B 2		2"	2½"	3½"	4½"
C 2		2"	2½"	3½"	4½"
C 1		2" x 5"	2½" x 6½"	3½" x 9½"	4½" x 12½"

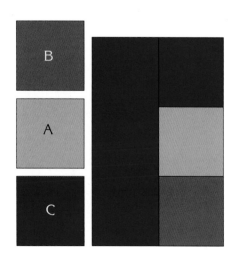

Hands of Friendship

QST—page 14
Adding Triangles to a Square—page 25

Color/Cut	Subcut	4½"	6"	9"	12"
A 4	▢	2"	2½"	3½"	4½"
A 1	⊠	2¾"	3¼"	4¼"	5¼"
B 1	⊠	2¾"	3¼"	4¼"	5¼"
B 1	⊠	2⅜"	2⅞"	3⅞"	4⅞""
C 1	⊠	2¾"	3¼"	4¼"	5¼"
C 1	⊠	2⅜"	2⅞"	3⅞"	4⅞"

TIPS
There will be one extra QST.

Hovering Hawks

HST—pages 12–13
Adding Triangles to a Square—page 25

Color/Cut	Subcut	4½"	6"	9"	12"
A 2	◺	2⅜"	2⅞"	3⅞"	4⅞"
B 6	◺	1⅝"	1⅞"	2⅜"	2⅞"
C 2	◺	1⅝"	1⅞"	2⅜"	2⅞"
C 5	▢	2"	2½"	3½"	4½"

TIPS
Make the B/C small half-square triangles first.
Then sew the other B triangles to either side of the HST.
Add an A triangle to complete unit.

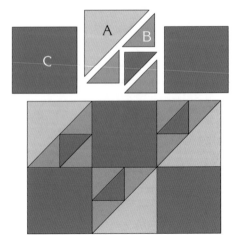

Indian Puzzle

HST—pages 12–13
Square-in-a-Square—page 23

Color/Cut	Subcut	4½"	6"	9"	12"
A 1		2"	2½"	3½"	4½"
A 4	◹	2⅜"	2⅞"	3⅞"	4⅞"
B 4	◹	2⅜"	2⅞"	3⅞"	4⅞"
B 4		1¼"	1½"	2"	2½"

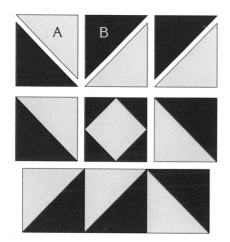

King's Crown

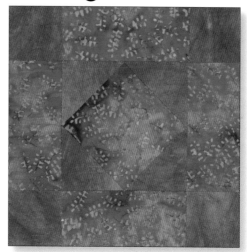

Square-in-a-Square—page 23

Color/Cut	Subcut	4½"	6"	9"	12"
A 1		2¾"	3½"	5"	6½"
A 4		1⅝" x 2¾"	2" x 3½"	2¾" x 5"	3½" x 6½"
B 8		1⅝"	2"	2¾"	3½"

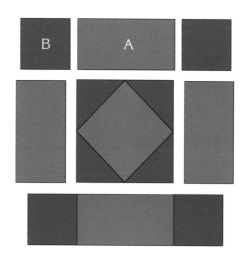

Ladies Aid Album

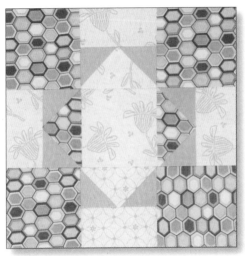

Flying Geese from Squares—page 17

Color/Cut	Subcut	4½"	6"	9"	12"
A 1		2"	2½"	3½"	4½"
*A 6		1¼" x 2"	1½" x 2½"	2" x 3½"	2½" x 4½"
*B 8		1¼"	1½"	2"	2½"
C 4		2"	2½"	3½"	4½"
*C 2		1¼" x 2"	1½" x 2½"	2" x 3½"	2½" x 4½"

---TIPS---
*Use 2, A & C rectangles and B squares to make Flying Geese from Squares on page 17.

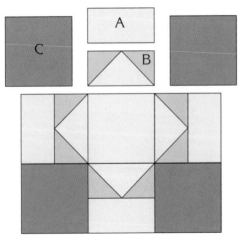

Massachusetts Block

HST—pages 12–13
QST—page 14

Color/Cut	Subcut	4½"	6"	9"	12"
A 1		2"	2½"	3½"	4½"
A 2	◻	2⅜"	2⅞"	3⅞"	4⅞"
A 2	⊠	2¾"	3¼"	4¼"	5¼"
B 1		2"	2½"	3½"	4½"
B 2	◻	2⅜"	2⅞"	3⅞"	4⅞"
B 2	⊠	2¾"	3¼"	4¼"	5¼"

---TIPS---
There will be triangles left over from A & B HST subcuts.

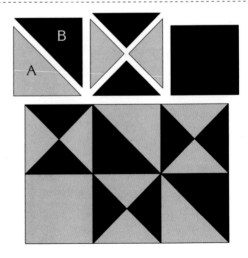

Mississippi Block

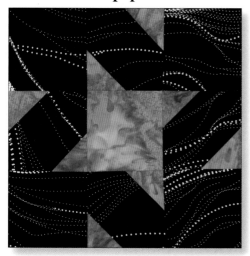

Adding Corners—page 24

Color/Cut	Subcut	4½"	6"	9"	12"
A 1		2"	2½"	3½"	4½"
*A 8		1¼"	1½"	2"	2½"
*B 8		2"	2½"	3½"	4½"

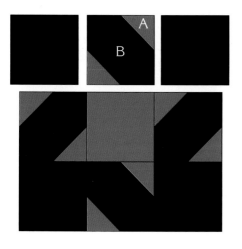

Monkey Wrench

HST—pages 12–13

Color/Cut	Subcut	4½"	6"	9"	12"
A 1		2"	2½"	3½"	4½"
A 2		2⅜"	2⅞"	3⅞"	4⅞"
A 4		1¼" x 2"	1½" x 2½"	2" x 3½"	2½" x 4½"
B 2		2⅜"	2⅞"	3⅞"	4⅞"
B 4		1¼" x 2"	1½" x 2½"	2" x 3½"	2½" x 4½"

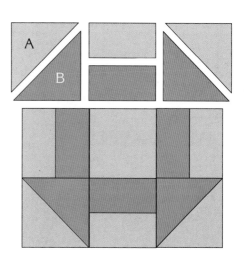

Mosaic 14 Block

Flying Geese from Squares—page 17
Square-in-a-Square—page 23

Color/Cut	Subcut	4½"	6"	9"	12"
*A 16		1⅝"	2"	2¾"	3½"
B 2		2¾"	2¾"	5"	6½"
*B 7		1⅝" x 2¾"	2" x 3½"	2¾" x 5"	3½" x 6½"

───TIPS───
*Use 6-A squares and 3-B rectangles to make Flying Geese
from Squares on page 17.

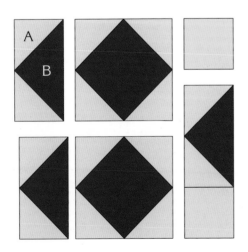

Mystery Garden

HST—pages 12–13
QST—page 15

Color/Cut	Subcut	4½"	6"	9"	12"
A 1	⊠	2¾"	3¼"	4¼"	5¼"
B 1		2"	2½"	3½"	4½"
B 2	⊠	2¾"	3¼"	4¼"	5¼"
C 2	⊠	2¾"	3¼"	4¼"	5¼"
C 2	⊠	2⅜"	2⅞"	3⅞"	4⅞"
D 1	⊠	2¾"	3¼"	4¼"	5¼"

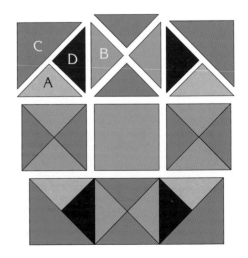

Night Vision

Flying Geese from Triangles—page 16
Partial Seams—page 20

Color/Cut		Subcut	4½"	6"	9"	12"
A 2		◹	2⅜"	2⅞"	3⅞"	4⅞"
B 1			2"	2½"	3½"	4½"
B 2		◹	2⅜"	2⅞"	3⅞"	4⅞"
C 1		⊠	5¼"	5¼"	7¼"	9¼"

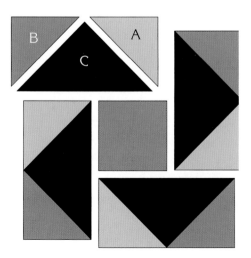

Nine Patch

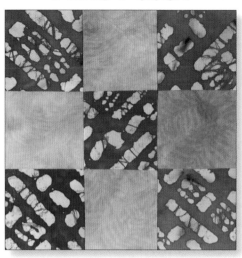

Color/Cut		Subcut	4½"	6"	9"	12"
A 4			2"	2½"	3½"	4½"
B 5			2"	2½"	3½"	4½"

---TIPS---
This nine patch is a simple beginner block,
good for practicing accurate seams.

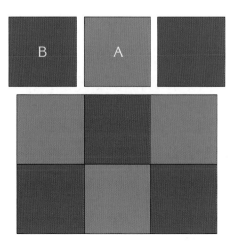

Nine Patch Variation

Color/Cut	Subcut	4½"	6"	9"	12"
A 4	⬜	1⅝" x 2¾"	2" x 3½"	2¾" x 5"	3½" x 6½"
B 1	⬛	2¾"	3½"	5"	6½"
B 4	⬛	1⅝"	2"	2¾"	3½"

────TIPS────
A Nine Patch can have unequal sized pieces as long
as it has nine parts. (See Nine Patch page 65.)

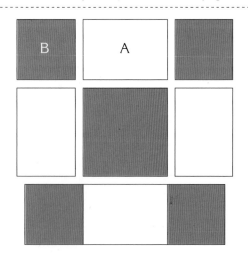

North Wind

Triangles-in-a-Row—pages 26–27

Color/Cut	Subcut	4½"	6"	9"	12"
A 1	◺	3⅞"	4⅞"	6⅞"	8⅞"
A 3	◺	2⅜"	2⅞"	3⅞"	4⅞"
B 1	◺	3⅞"	4⅞"	6⅞"	8⅞"
B 3	◺	2⅜"	2⅞"	3⅞"	4⅞"

────TIPS────
There will be triangles left over from A & B HST subcuts.

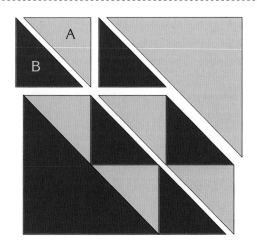

Ohio Star

QST—page 14

Color/Cut	Subcut	4½"	6"	9"	12"
A 5 ▢		2"	2½"	3½"	4½"
A 1 ▢	⊠	2¾"	3¼"	4¼"	5¼"
B 2 ▦	⊠	2¾"	3¼"	4¼"	5¼"
C 1 ■	⊠	2¾"	3¼"	4¼"	5¼"

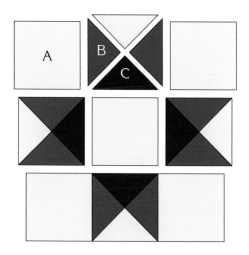

Old Maid's Puzzle

HST—pages 12–13

Color/Cut	Subcut	4½"	6"	9"	12"
A 3 ▧	◺	2⅜"	2⅞"	3⅞"	4⅞"
B 3 ▦	◺	2⅜"	2⅞"	3⅞"	4⅞"
B 3 ▦		2"	2½"	3½"	4½"

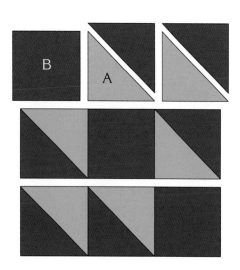

The 3 x 3 Grid Blocks

Puss In The Corner

HST—pages 12–13;

Color/Cut	Subcut	4½"	6"	9"	12"
A 1	⬜	2½"	4½"	6½"	8½"
B 2	◪ ◺	1⅝"	1⅞"	2⅜"	2⅞"
C 2	◪ ◺	1⅝"	1⅞"	2⅜"	2⅞"
C 4	▭	1¼" x 3½"	2" x 4½"	2½" x 6½"	3" x 8½"

─── TIPS ───
This could be a great setting block to alternate with more intricate 3 and 6 grid blocks.

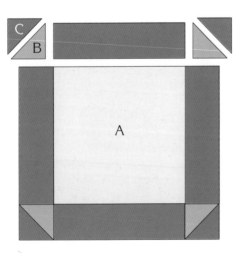

Rail Fence

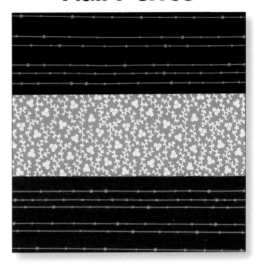

Color/Cut	Subcut	4½"	6"	9"	12"
A 2	⬛	2" x 5"	2½" x 6½"	3½" x 9½"	4½" x 12½"
B 1	▨	2" x 5"	2½" x 6½"	3½" x 9½"	4½" x 12½"

─── TIPS ───
It's a simple block. Alternate blocks horizontally and vertically for an easy, quick quilt.

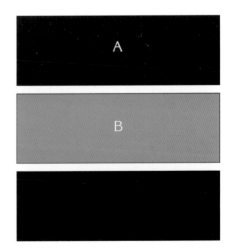

Ribbon Quilt

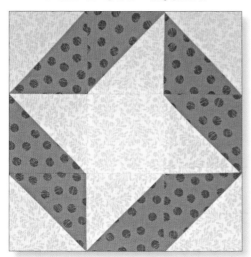

HST—pages 12–13

Color/Cut	Subcut	4½"	6"	9"	12"
A 1		2"	2½"	3½"	4½"
A 4	◹	2⅜"	2⅞"	3⅞"	4⅞"
B 4	◹	2⅜"	2⅞"	3⅞"	4⅞"

---TIPS---
Pay attention to the orientation of HSTs when sewing
this block together.

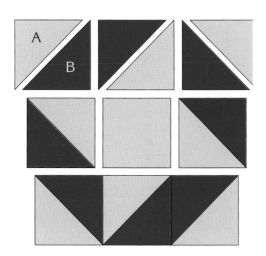

Rocky Road To California

HST—pages 12–13

Color/Cut	Subcut	4½"	6"	9"	12"
A 2	◹	2⅜"	2⅞"	3⅞"	4⅞"
B 2	◹	2⅜"	2⅞"	3⅞"	4⅞"
B 6		1¼"	1½"	2"	2½"
C 6		1¼"	1½"	2"	2½"
C 2		2"	2½"	3½"	4½"

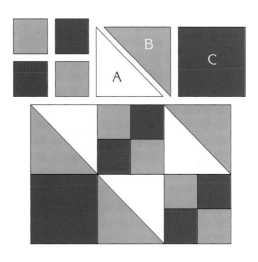

Rolling Stone Block

Square-in-a-Square—page 23

Color/Cut	Subcut	4½"	6"	9"	12"
A 5		2"	2½"	3½"	4½"
A 4		1¼" x 2"	1½" x 2½"	2" x 3½"	2½" x 4½"
B 4		1¼" x 2"	1½" x 2½"	2" x 3½"	2½" x 4½"
B 16		1¼"	1½"	2"	2½"

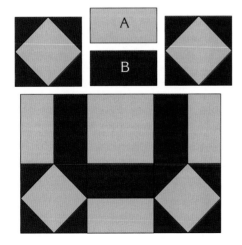

Roundabout Block

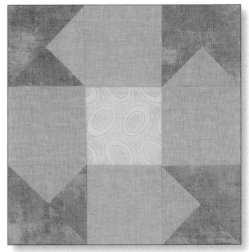

HST—pages 12–13
QST—page 14 (steps 1–4)

Color/Cut	Subcut	4½"	6"	9"	12"
A 1		2"	2½"	3½"	4½"
B 1	⊠	2¾"	3¼"	4¼"	5¼"
C 1	⊠	2¾"	3¼"	4¼"	5¼"
C 2	⊠	2⅜"	2⅞"	3⅞"	4⅞"

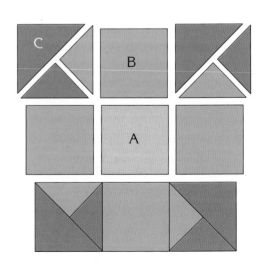

Sail Boat

HST—pages 12–13
Adding Triangles to a Square—page 25

Color/Cut	Subcut	4½"	6"	9"	12"
A 3		2⅜"	2⅞"	3⅞"	4⅞"
A 1		3⅜"	4⅞"	6⅞"	8⅞"
B 4		2⅜"	2⅞"	3⅞"	4⅞"
C 1		2"	2½"	3½"	4½"

---TIPS---
There will be triangles left over from A & B HST subcuts.

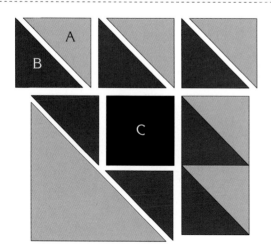

Split Nine Patch

HST—pages 12–13

Color/Cut	Subcut	4½"	6"	9"	12"
A 2		2"	2½"	3½"	4½"
A 3		2⅜"	2⅞"	3⅞"	4⅞"
B 1		2"	2½"	3½"	4½"
B 3			2⅞"	3⅞"	4⅞"

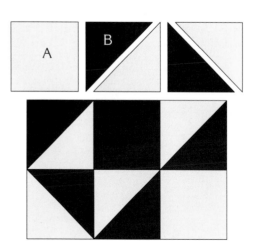

The 3 x 3 Grid Blocks

Sunset Light

Color/Cut	Subcut	4½"	6"	9"	12"
A 2	☐	2"	2½"	3½"	4½"
A 2	▭	1¼" x 2"	1½" x 2½"	2" x 3½"	2½" x 4½"
B 4	◼	2"	2½"	3½"	4½"
C 4	◼	1¼"	1½"	2"	2½"
D 4	◼	1¼"	1½"	2"	2½"

─── TIPS ───
Try using solid colors for the components in this block. Experiment with your favorite colors for a more contemporary look.

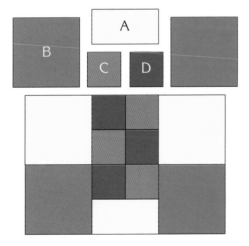

The Letter X

QST—pages 14–15

Color/Cut	Subcut	4½"	6"	9"	12"
A 3	☐ ⊠	2¾"	3¼"	4¼"	5¼"
B 3	◼ ⊠	2¾"	3¼"	4¼"	5¼"
C 4	◼	2"	2½"	3½"	4½"

─── TIPS ───
There will be triangles left over from A & B QST subcuts.

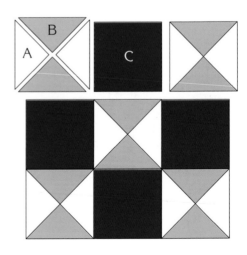

The Practical Orchard

HST—pages 12–13
QST—page 14

Color/Cut	Subcut		4½"	6"	9"	12"
A 2			2"	2½"	3½"	4½"
A 2		◻	2⅜"	2⅞"	3⅞"	4⅞"
A 1		⊠	2¾"	3¼"	4¼"	5¼"
B 2			2"	2½"	3½"	4½"
B 2		◻	2⅜"	2⅞"	3⅞"	4⅞"
B 1		⊠	2¾"	3¼"	4¼"	5¼"

> ___ TIPS ___
> There will be triangles left over from A & B QST subcuts.

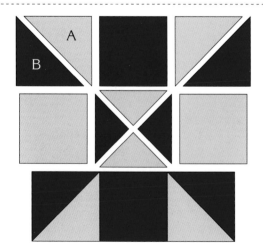

The Railroad

HST—pages 12–13

Color/Cut	Subcut		4½"	6"	9"	12"
A 10			1¼"	1½"	2"	2½"
A 2		◻	2⅜"	2⅞"	3⅞8"	4⅞"
B 10			1¼"	1½"	2"	2½"
C 2		◻	2⅜"	2⅞"	3⅞"	4⅞"

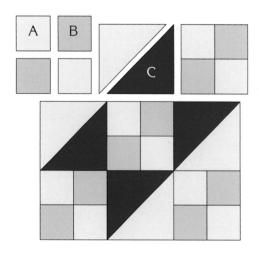

Three and Six Block

HST—pages 12–13

Color/Cut	Subcut	4½"	6"	9"	12"
A 2		2⅜"	2⅞"	3⅞"	4⅞"
B 1		2⅜"	2⅞"	3⅞"	4⅞"
B 1		2"	2½"	3½"	4½"
C 2		2"	2½"	3½"	4½"
D 3		2⅜"	2⅞"	3⅞"	4⅞"

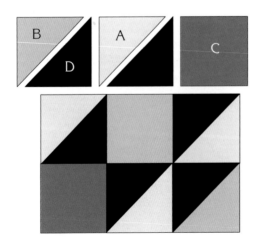

Toy Windmill

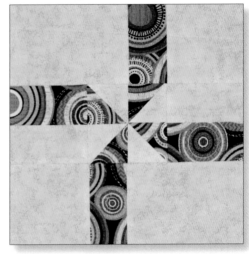

HST—pages 12–13

Color/Cut	Subcut	4½"	6"	9"	12"
A 2		1¼" x 2"	1½" x 2½"	2" x 3½"	2½" x 4½"
A 2		1⅝"	1⅞"	2⅜"	2⅞"
A 2		2 "x 2¾"	2½" x 3½"	3½" x 5"	4½" x 6½"
A 2		2"	2½"	3½"	4½"
B 2		1⅝"	1⅞"	2⅜"	2⅞"
B 4		1¼" x 2"	1½" x 2½"	2" x 3½"	2½" x 4½"

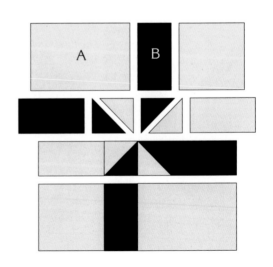

Twin Sisters

QST—page 14
Adding Corners—page 24

Color/Cut		Subcut	4½"	6"	9"	12"
A 1	[square]	[triangle]	2"	3⅞"	5⅜"	6⅞"
*A 2	[rectangle]		1⅝ x 2¾	2" x 3½"	2¾" x 5"	3½" x 6½"
A 1	[square]	[triangle]	2"	2⅜"	3⅛"	3⅞"
B 1	[square]	[triangle]	2"	3⅞"	5⅜"	6⅞"
*B 2	[rectangle]		1⅝" x 2¾"	2" x 3½"	2¾" x 5"	3½" x 6½"
B 1	[square]	[triangle]	2"	2⅜"	3⅛"	3⅞"
C 2	[square]	[triangle]	2"	2⅜"	3⅛"	3⅞"
*C 4	[square]		1⅝"	2"	2¾"	3½"

TIPS
*For Adding Corners, page 24,
use rectangles and 4-C squares.

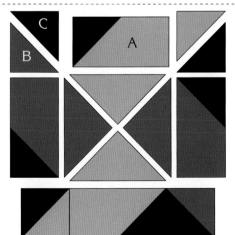

Twin Star

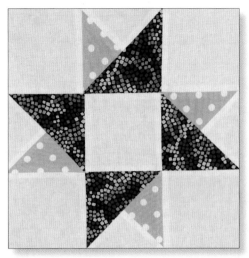

HST—pages 12–13
QST—page 14 (steps 1–4)

Color/Cut		Subcut	4½"	6"	9"	12"
A 5	[square]		2"	2½"	3½"	4½"
A 1	[square]	[X subcut]	2¾"	3¼"	4¼"	5¼"
B 1	[square]	[X subcut]	2¾"	3¼"	4¼"	5¼"
C 2	[square]	[triangle]	2⅜"	2⅞"	3⅞"	4⅞"

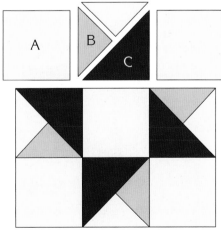

The 3 x 3 Grid Blocks

The 4 x 4 Grid Blocks

The 4 x 4 grid is really interesting to me; more squares = more detail. Half-square triangles are used repeatedly in many of the blocks, but patterns made by turning, flipping, and repeating them give the blocks a personality of their own. Half-square triangles can make flying geese and pinwheels. It's all in the way they are oriented.

Aircraft Block

HST—pages 12–13
Adding Triangles to a Square—page 25
Adding Corners—page 24

Color/Cut		Subcut	4½"	6"	9"	12"
A 1		◨	3⅛"	3⅞"	5⅞"	6⅞"
A 5		◩	2"	2⅜"	3⅛"	3⅞"
B 2		◩	3⅛"	3⅞"	5⅜"	6⅞"
C 2		◨	2"	2⅜"	3⅛"	3⅞"
*C 1			1⅝"	2"	2¾"	3½"

--- TIPS ---
*Add the C square to the corner of the HST, lower left.

There will be triangles left over from A & C HST subcuts.

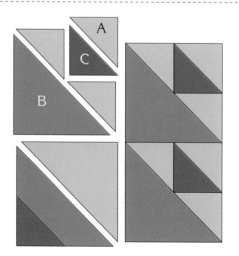

Angela's Star

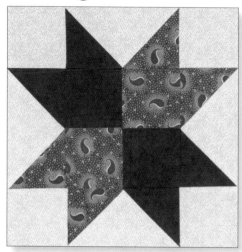

Flying Geese from Squares—page 17

Color/Cut		Subcut	4½"	6"	9"	12"
A 4			1⅝"	2"	2¾"	3½"
*A 4			1⅝" x 2¾"	2" x 3½"	2¾" x 5"	3½" x 6½"
*B 6			1⅝"	2"	2¾"	3½"
*C 6			1⅝"	2"	2¾"	3½"

--- TIPS ---
*Use 4-B & C squares, and 4-A rectangles to make Flying Geese from Squares, page 17.

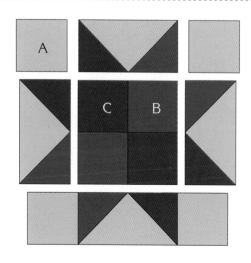

Bachelor's Puzzle

Parallel Seams—page 22
Square-in-a-Square—page 23

Color/Cut	Subcut	4½"	6"	9"	12"
A 4		1⅝"	2"	2¾"	3½"
B 1		2¾"	3½"	5"	6½"
*C 4		1⅝" x 2¾"	2" x 3½"	2¾" x 5"	3½" x 6½"
*D 12		1⅝"	2"	2¾"	3½"

TIPS
*Use C rectangles and 8-D squares to
make parallel blocks, page 22.

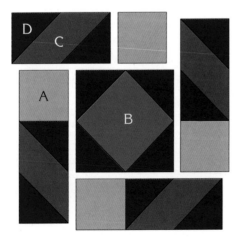

Balkan Puzzle

HST—pages 12–13
Flying Geese from Squares—page 17
Square-in-a-Square—page 23

Color/Cut	Subcut	4½"	6"	9"	12"
*A 4		1⅝"	2"	2¾"	3½"
A 2		2"	2⅜"	3⅛"	3⅞"
*B 4		1⅝" x 2¾"	2" x 3½"	2¾" x 5"	3½" x 6½"
C 2		2"	2⅜"	3⅛"	3⅞"
*C 8		1⅝"	2"	2¾"	3½"
C 1		2¾"	3½"	5"	6½"

TIPS
*Use 4-A & C squares, and 4-B rectangles
to make Flying Geese from Squares, page 17.

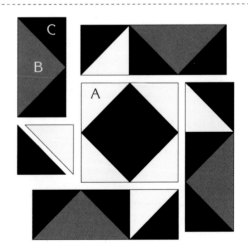

Brave World

HST—pages 12–13
Adding Triangles to a Square—page 25

Color/Cut	Subcut		4½"	6"	9"	12"
A 4		◹	2"	2⅜"	3⅛"	3⅞"
B 4			1⅝"	2"	2¾"	3½"
C 2		◹	3⅛"	3⅞"	5⅜"	6⅞"

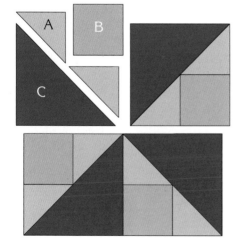

Brown Goose

Four-at-a-Time Flying Geese—page 18

Color/Cut	Subcut	4½"	6"	9"	12"
*A 1		3½"	4¼"	5¾"	7¼"
**A 4		2	2⅜"	3⅛"	3⅞"
**B 1		3½"	4¼"	5¾"	7¼"
*B 4		2	2⅜"	3⅛"	3⅞"

---TIPS---
* Use the large A square and 4-B squares to make Four-at-a-Time Flying Geese, page 18.

**Use the large B square and 4-A squares to make Four-at-a-Time Flying Geese, page 18.

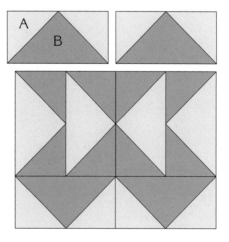

Cheyenne Block

HST—pages 12–13
Square-in-a-Square—page 23

Color/Cut	Subcut		4½"	6"	9"	12"
A 1	□		2¾"	3½"	5"	6½"
A 2	□	◨	2"	2⅜"	3⅛"	3⅞"
B 6	▨		1⅝"	2"	2¾"	3½"
B 1	▨	◨	2"	2⅜"	3⅛"	3⅞"
C 6	▨		1⅝"	2"	2¾"	3½"
C 1	▨	◨	2"	2⅜"	3⅛"	3⅞"

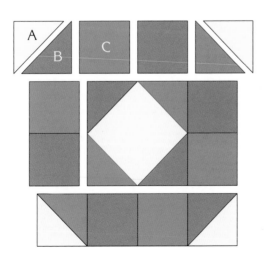

Clay's Choice

HST—pages 12–13

Color/Cut	Subcut		4½"	6"	9"	12"
A 4	□		1⅝"	2"	2¾"	3½"
A 4	□	◨	2"	2⅜"	3⅛"	3⅞"
B 4	▨		1⅝"	2"	2¾"	3½"
C 4	■	◨	2"	2⅜"	3⅛"	3⅞"

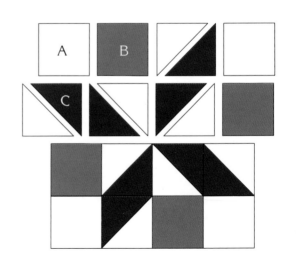

Clay's Choice Variation

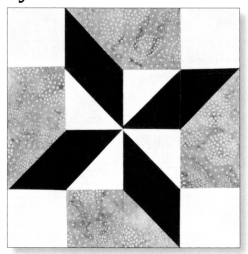

HST—pages 12–13

Color/Cut	Subcut	4½"	6"	9"	12"
A 4		1⅝"	2"	2¾"	3½"
A 2	◺	2"	2⅜"	3⅛"	3⅞"
B 4		1⅝"	2"	2¾"	3½"
B 2	◺	2"	2⅜"	3⅛"	3⅞"
C 4	◺	2"	2⅜"	3⅛"	3⅞"

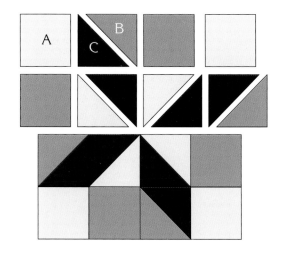

Colorado Beauty

HST—pages 12–13
Four-at-a-Time Flying Geese—page 18

Color/Cut	Subcut	4½"	6"	9"	12"
A 4	◺	2"	2⅜"	3⅛"	3⅞"
*A 1		3½"	4¼"	5¾"	7¼"
*B 4		2"	2⅜"	3⅛"	3⅞"
B 4	◺	2"	2⅜"	3⅛"	3⅞"

TIPS
*Use the large A square and 4-B squares to make Four-at-a-Time Flying Geese, page 18.

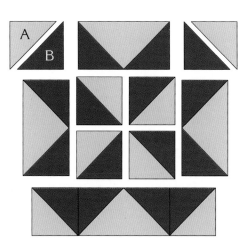

Crossed Paths

Four-at-a-Time Flying Geese—page 18
Adding Corners—page 24

Color/Cut	Subcut	4½"	6"	9"	12"
**A 1		2¾"	3½"	5"	6½"
*A 4		2"	2⅜"	3⅛"	3⅞"
*B 1		3½"	4¼"	5¾"	7½"
B 2		1⅝"	2"	2¾"	3½"
**C 4		1⅝"	2"	2¾"	3½"

TIPS

*Use the large B square and 4-A squares to make
Four-at-a-Time Flying Geese, page 18.

**For Adding Corners, page 24,
use large A block and 2-C blocks.

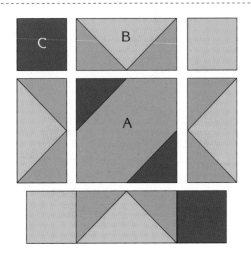

Double Four-Patch

HST—pages 12–13

Color/Cut	Subcut	4½"	6"	9"	12"
A 1	◹	3⅛"	3⅞"	5"	6⅞"
A 4		1⅝"	2"	2¾"	3½"
B 1	◹	3⅝"	3⅞"	5"	6⅞"
B 4		1⅝"	2"	2¾"	3½"

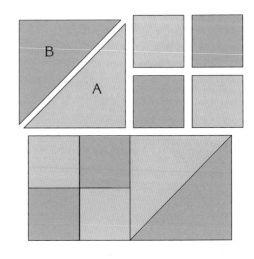

Double Quartet

HST—pages 12–13

Color/Cut	Subcut	4½"	6"	9"	12"
A 4		1⅝"	2"	2¾"	3½"
A 4		2"	2⅜"	3⅛"	3⅞"
B 4		1⅝"	2"	2¾"	3½"
B 4		2"	2⅜"	3⅛"	3⅞"

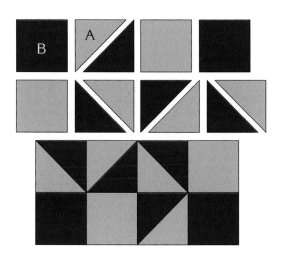

Dutchman's Puzzle

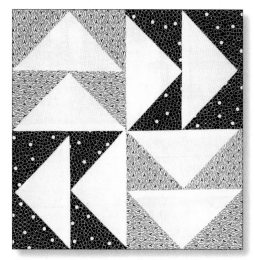

Four-at-a-Time Flying Geese—page 18

Color/Cut	Subcut	4½"	6"	9"	12"
*A 2		3½"	4¼"	5¾"	7¾"
*B 4		2"	2⅜"	3⅛"	3⅞"
*C 4		2"	2⅜"	3⅛"	3⅞"

---TIPS---
Note: The 2-A squares are for "geese"
bodies and the B & C squares are for "sky" to make
Four-at-a-Time Flying Geese, page 18.

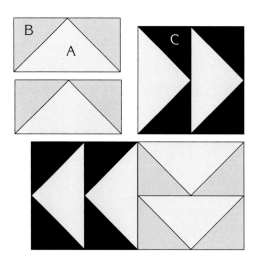

The 4 x 4 Grid Blocks

Fancy Corners

HST—pages 12–13
QST—page 14 (steps 1–4)
Adding Corners—page 24

Color/Cut	Subcut	4½"	6"	9"	12"
*A 1	☐	2¾"	3½"	5"	6½"
A 4	☐	1⅝"	2"	2¾"	3½"
A 3	☐ ◩	2"	2⅜"	3⅛"	3⅞"
B 1	▨ ⊠	2⅜"	2¾"	3½"	4¼"
C 1	▨ ⊠	2⅜"	2¾"	3½"	4¼"
*D 2	▨	1⅝"	2"	2¾"	3½"
D 4	▨ ◩	2"	2⅜"	3⅛"	3⅞"

TIPS
For Adding Corners, page 24,
use large A square and 2-D squares.
There will be triangles left over from B & C QST subcuts.

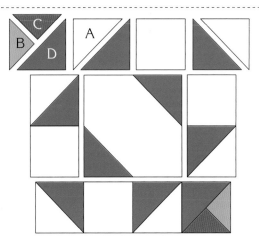

Fishing Boats

HST—pages 12–13

Color/Cut	Subcut	4½"	6"	9"	12"
A 3	☐ ◩	2"	2⅜"	3⅛"	3⅞"
A 1	▭	1⅝" x 2¾"	2" x 3½"	2¾" x 5"	3½" x 6½"
A 2	▭	1⅝" x 3⅞"	2" X 5"	2¾" X 7¼"	3½" X 9½"
B 1	▬	1⅝" x2¾"	2" x 3½"	2¾" x 5"	3½" x 6½"
B 3	▬ ◩	2"	2⅜"	3⅛"	3⅞"

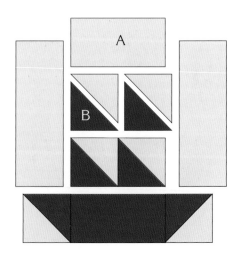

Flower Basket

HST—pages 12–13

Color/Cut	Subcut		4½"	6"	9"	12"
A 4		◹	2"	2⅜"	3⅛"	3⅞"
B 2			1⅝" x 2¾"	2" x 3½"	2¾" x 5"	3½" x 6½"
B 1			1⅝"	2"	2¾"	3½"
B 1		◹	2"	2⅜"	3⅛"	3⅞"
C 1			1⅝"	2"	2¾"	3½"
C 3		◹	2"	2⅜"	3⅛"	3⅞"
D 2		◹	2"	2⅜"	3⅛"	3⅞"

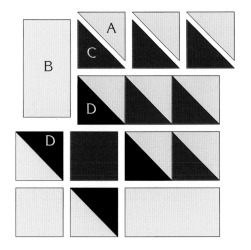

Four by Four Block

Adding Triangles to a Square—page 25

Color/Cut	Subcut		4½"	6"	9"	12"
A 4			1⅝"	2"	2¾"	3½"
B 1			3⅝"	4¾"	6⅞"	9"
C 4		◺	2	2⅜"	3⅛"	3⅞"

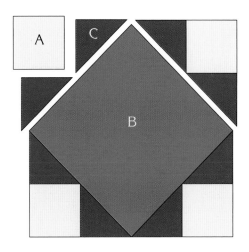

Free Trade

HST—pages 12–13
Flying Geese from Squares—page 17

Color/Cut	Subcut	4½"	6"	9"	12"
*A 6		1⅝" x 2¾"	2" X 3½"	2¾" X 5"	3½" X 6½"
A 6		1⅝"	2"	2¾"	3¾"
A 1		2"	2⅜"	3⅛"	3⅞"
B 1		2"	2⅜"	3⅛"	3⅞"
*B 8		1⅝"	2"	2¾"	3½"

TIPS
*Use the A rectangles and B squares to make
Flying Geese from Squares, page 17.

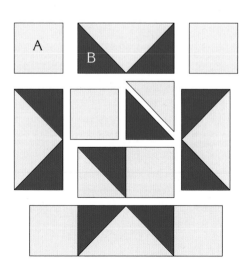

Girl's Favorite

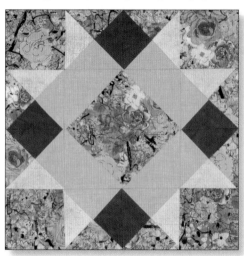

QST—page 14
Square-in-a-Square—page 23

Color/Cut	Subcut	4½"	6"	9"	12"
A 2		2⅜"	2¾"	3½"	4¼"
B 2		2⅜"	2¾"	3½"	4¼"
B 4		1⅝"	2"	2¾"	3½"
C 2		2⅜"	2¾"	3½"	4¼"
C 1		2¾	3½"	5"	6½"
C 4		1⅝"	2"	2¾"	3½"
D 2		2⅜"	2¾"	3½"	4¼"

TIPS
Note: There are 41 pieces in this block. Have no fear! Just
lay out the pieces before you start sewing.

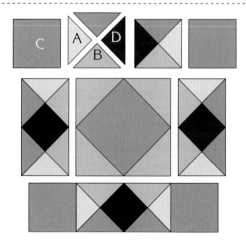

Indian Hatchet

HST—pages 12–13

Color/Cut	Subcut	4½"	6"	9"	12"
A 2 ⬜		1⅝"	2"	2¾"	3½"
A 4 ⬜	◺	2"	2⅜"	3⅛"	3⅞"
B 1 ⬛		2¾"	3½"	5"	6½"
C 4 ⬛	◺	2"	2⅜"	3⅛"	3⅞"
C 2 ⬛		1⅝"	2"	2¾"	3½"

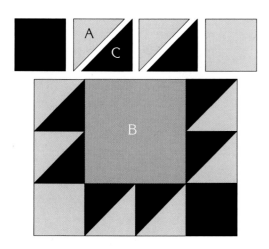

Jack in the Box

HST—pages 12–13
Flying Geese from Squares—page 17

Color/Cut	Subcut	4½"	6"	9"	12"
*A 6 ⬜		1⅝" x 2¾"	2" X 3½"	2¾" X 5"	3½" X 6½"
A 2 ⬜	◹		2"	2⅜"	3⅛"	3⅞"
B 2 ⬛	◹		2"	2⅜"	3⅛"	3⅞"
*B 12 ⬛		1⅝"	2"	2¾"	3½"

----- TIPS -----
*Use A rectangles and B squares to make
Flying Geese from Squares on page 17.

Marion's Choice

HST—pages 12–13
QST—pages 14–15
Adding Triangles to a Square—page 25

Color/Cut	Subcut		4½"	6"	9"	12"
A 1	☐	⊠	3½"	4¼"	5¾"	7¼"
A 2	☐	◻	2"	2⅜"	3⅛"	3⅞"
A 2	☐	⊠	2⅜"	2¾"	3½"	4¼"
B 1	■	⊠	3½"	4¼"	5¾"	7¼"
B 2	■	◻	2"	2⅜"	3⅛"	3⅞"
B 1	■	⊠	2⅜"	2¾"	3½"	4¼"

---TIPS---
Note: Referring to illustration below and paying close
attention to color orientation, make QSTs first. Add small
A and B triangles to two sides of each QST. Add large A/B
triangle sets to finish the "square."

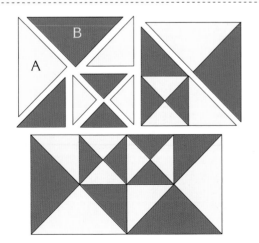

Mill Wheel Block

HST—pages 12–13
Square-in-a-Square—page 23

Color/Cut	Subcut		4½"	6"	9"	12"
A 8	■		1⅝"	2"	2¾"	3½"
A 4	■	◿	2"	2⅜"	3⅛"	3⅞"
B 4	■	◿	2"	2⅜"	3⅛"	3⅞"
C 1	■		2¾"	3½"	5"	6½"

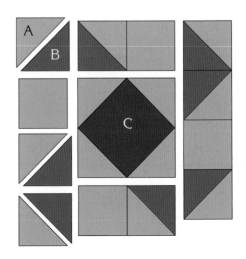

Mosaic 6 Block

HST—pages 12–13
Square-in-a-Square—page 23

Color/Cut	Subcut	4½"	6"	9"	12"
A 1		2¾"	3½"	5"	6½"
A 6		2"	2⅜"	3⅛"	3⅞"
B 6		2"	2⅜"	3⅛"	3⅞"
B 4		1⅝"	2"	2¾"	3½"

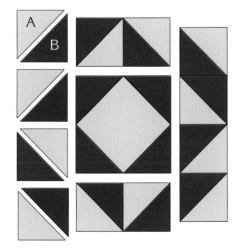

Mosaic 9 Block

HST—pages 12–13

Color/Cut	Subcut	4½"	6"	9"	12"
A 8		2"	2⅜"	3⅛"	3⅞"
B 4		2"	2⅜"	3⅛"	3⅞"
C 4		2"	2⅜"	3⅛"	3⅞"

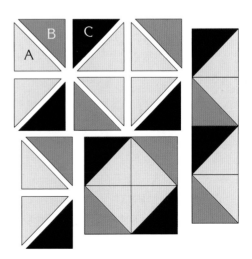

Mosaic 10 Block

Flying Geese from Squares—page 17
Square-in-a-Square—page 23

Color/Cut	Subcut	4½"	6"	9"	12"
*A 8		1⅝"	2"	2¾"	3½"
*A 2		1⅝" x 2¾"	2" x 3½"	2¾" x 5"	3½" x 6½"
B 1		2¾"	3½"	5"	6½"
C 4		1⅝"	2"	2¾"	3½""
*D 4		1⅝" x 2¾"	2" x 3½"	2¾" x 5"	3½" x 6½"
*D 4		1⅝"	2"	2¾"	3½"

--- TIPS ---
*Use 8-A squares/4-D rectangles, and 2-A rectangles/4-D
squares to make Flying Geese from Squares, page 17.

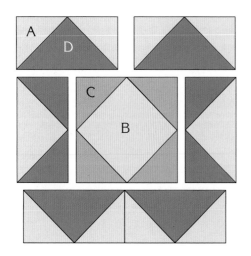

Mosaic 12 Block

Four-at-a-Time Flying Geese—page 18

Color/Cut	Subcut	4½"	6"	9"	12"
*A 8		2"	2⅜"	3⅛"	3⅞"
*B 1		3½"	4¼"	5¾"	7¼"
*C 1		3½"	4¼"	5¾"	7¼"

--- TIPS ---
Note: Use B & C squares for "geese" bodies and
A squares are for "sky" to make
Four-at-a-Time Flying Geese, page 18.

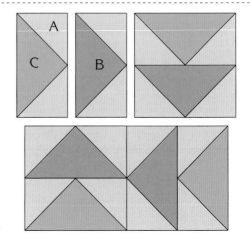

Mosaic 13 Block

HST—pages 12–13
Flying Geese From Squares—page 17
Geese have light and dark "sky" triangles.

Color/Cut	Subcut	4½"	6"	9"	12"
*A 4	☐	1⅝"	2"	2¾"	3½"
A 2	◺	2"	2⅜"	3⅛"	3⅞"
B 2	◺	2"	2⅜"	3⅛"	3⅞"
*B 4	☐	1⅝"	2"	2¾"	3½"
*C 4	▭	1⅝" x 2¾"	2" x 3½"	2¾" x 5"	3½" x 6½"
D 2	◺	2"	2⅜"	3⅛"	3⅞"
E 2	◺	2"	2⅜"	3⅛"	3⅞"

------ TIPS ------
*Use A & B squares and C rectangles to
make Flying Geese from Squares, page 17.

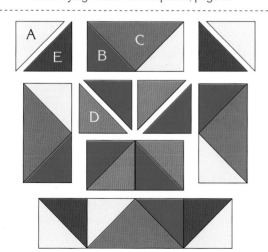

Mosaic 13 Variation

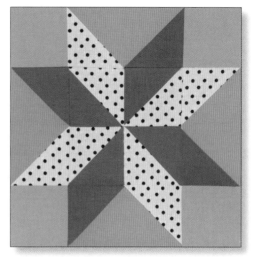

HST—pages 12–13
Flying Geese From Squares—page 17
Geese have light and dark "sky" triangles.

Color/Cut	Subcut	4½"	6"	9"	12"
*A 4	☐	1⅝"	2"	2¾"	3½"
A 2	◺	2"	2⅜"	3⅛"	3⅞"
B 4	☐	1⅝"	2"	2¾"	3½"
*C 4	▭	1⅝" x 2¾"	2" x 3½"	2¾" x 5"	3½" x 6½"
*D 4	☐	1⅝"	2"	2¾"	3½"
D 2	◺	2"	2⅜"	3⅛"	3⅞"

------ TIPS ------
*Use A & D squares and C rectangles to
make Flying Geese from Squares, page 17.

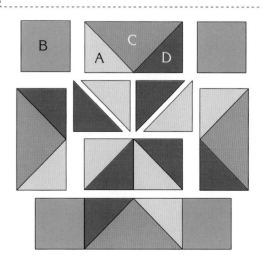

The 4 x 4 Grid Blocks

Mosaic 17 Block

HST—pages 12–13

Color/Cut	Subcut	4½"	6"	9"	12"
A 8	⬜ ◺	2"	2⅜"	3⅛"	3⅞"
B 8	◼ ◺	2"	2⅜"	3⅛"	3⅞"

assorted colors

─── TIPS ───
This is a good block to use up scraps and experiment with your own color combinations.

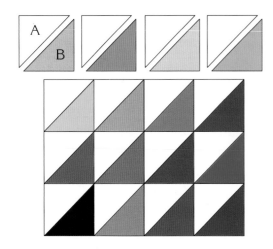

Mosaic 18 Block

HST—pages 12–13
Parallel Seams—page 22

Color/Cut	Subcut	4½"	6"	9"	12"
*A 8	◼	1⅝"	2"	2¾"	3½"
A 2	◼ ◺	2"	2⅜"	3⅛"	3⅞"
B 2	◼ ◺	2"	2⅜"	3⅛"	3⅞"
C 4	◼ ◺	2"	2⅜"	3⅛"	3⅞"
*D 4	◼	1⅝" x 2¾"	2" x 3½"	2¾" x 5"	3½" x 6½"

─── TIPS ───
*Use A squares and D rectangles to make Parallel Seams, page 22.

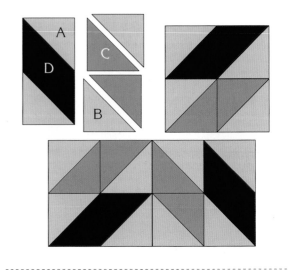

Mosaic 20 Block

HST—pages 12–13
Flying Geese from Squares—page 17
Square-in-a-Square—page 23

Color/Cut	Subcut	4½"	6"	9"	12"
A 2	◻◺	2"	2⅜"	3⅛"	3⅞"
A 1	◻	2¾"	3½"	5"	6½"
*A 8	◻	1⅝"	2"	2¾"	3½"
B 2	◻◺	2"	2⅜"	3⅛"	3⅞"
B 4	◻	1⅝"	2"	2¾"	3½"
*B 4	▭	1⅝" x 2¾"	2" x 3½"	2¾" x 5"	3½" x 6½"

```
┌──────────── TIPS ────────────┐
*Use A squares and B rectangles to make
   Flying Geese from Squares, page 17.
```

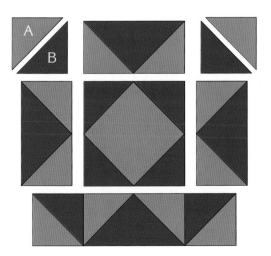

Mosaic 21 Block

HST—pages 12-13
Square-in-a-Square—page 23

Color/Cut	Subcut	4½"	6"	9"	12"
A 1	◻	2¾"	3½"	5"	6½"
A 6	◻◺	2"	2⅜"	3⅛"	3⅞"
B 2	◻	1⅝"	2"	2¾"	3½"
B 2	◻◺	2"	2⅜"	3⅛"	3⅞"
C 2	◻	1⅝"	2"	2¾"	3½"
C 2	◻◺	2"	2⅜"	3⅛"	3⅞"
D 2	◻◺	2"	2⅜"	3⅛"	3⅞"

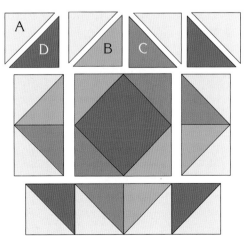

Mr. Roosevelt's Necktie

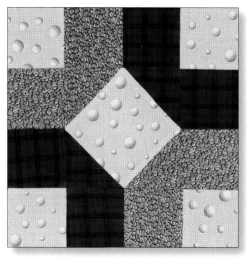

Square-in-a-Square—page 23

Color/Cut	Subcut	4½"	6"	9"	12"
A 1	▢	2¾"	3½"	5"	6½"
A 4	▢	1⅝"	2"	2¾"	3½"
B 6	▢	1⅝"	2"	2¾"	3½"
C 6	▢	1⅝"	2"	2¾"	3½"

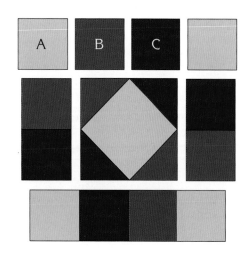

Navajo Block

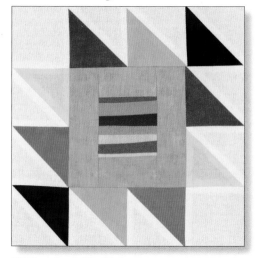

HST—pages 12–13

Color/Cut	Subcut	4½"	6"	9"	12"
A 2	▢	1⅝"	2"	2¾"	3½"
A 5	◨	2"	2⅜"	3⅛"	3⅞"
B 2	▭	1⅛" x 2¾"	1¼" x 3½"	1⅝" x 5"	2" x 6½"
B 2	▭	1⅛" x 1½"	1¼" x 2"	1⅝" x 2¾"	2" x 3½"
C 1	▪	1½"	2"	2¾"	3½"
D 5	◨	2"	2⅜"	3⅛"	3⅞"

TIPS

The "C" square was fussy cut from striped fabric.

For "D" squares use assorted colors.

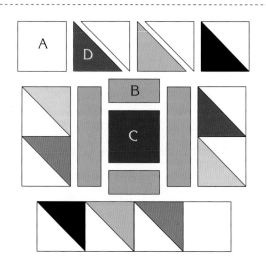

Old Tippecanoe

HST—pages 12–13

Color/Cut	Subcut	4½"	6"	9"	12"
A 8	◹	2"	2⅜"	3⅛"	3⅞"
B 4	◹	2"	2⅜"	3⅛"	3⅞"
C 4	◹	2"	2⅜"	3⅛"	3⅞"

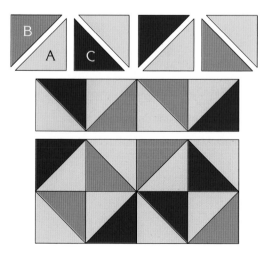

Our Editor

HST—pages 12–13
Flying Geese from Squares—page 17

Color/Cut	Subcut	4½"	6"	9"	12"
A 2	◹	2"	2⅜"	3⅛"	3⅞"
*A 2		1⅝" x 2¾"	2" x 3½"	2¾" x 5"	3½" x 6½"
*A 8		1⅝"	2"	2¾"	3½"
B 2	◹	2"	2⅜"	3⅛"	3⅞"
*B 4		1⅝" x 2¾"	2" x 3½"	2¾" x 5"	3½" x 6½"
*B 4		1⅝"	2"	2¾"	3½"

---TIPS---
*Use A squares/B rectangles, and B squares/A rectangles
to make Flying Geese from Squares, page 17.

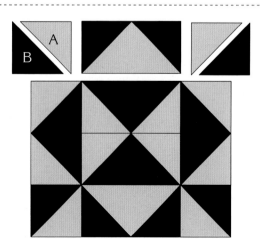

Pale Stars

Flying Geese From Squares—page 17

Color/Cut	Subcut	4½"	6"	9"	12"
*A 8		1⅝"	2"	2¾"	3½"
*B 4		1⅝"	2"	2¾"	3½"
*C 4		1⅝" x 2¾"	2" x 3½"	2¾" x 5"	3½" x 6½"
D 4		1⅝"	2"	2¾"	3½"

---TIPS---
*Use 4-A squares, 4-B squares and 4-C rectangles
to make Flying Geese from Squares, page 17.

Note: The center can also be
cut as a square; 3½", 5" or 6½."

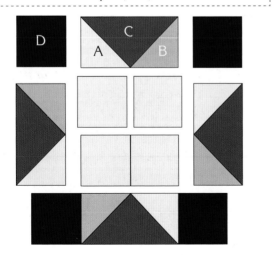

Path Through the Woods

HST—pages 12–13
Triangles-in-a-Row—page 26

Color/Cut	Subcut		4½"	6"	9"	12"
A 1			4¼"	5⅜"	7⅝"	9⅞"
A 4			2"	2⅜"	3⅛"	3⅞"
B 1			4¼"	5⅜"	7⅝"	9⅞"
B 4			2"	2⅜"	3⅛"	3⅞"

---TIPS---
There will be triangles left over from A & B HST subcuts.

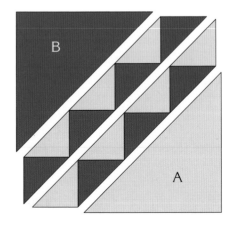

Patience Corners

HST—pages 12-13
Square-in-a-Square—page 23

Color/Cut	Subcut	4½"	6"	9"	12"
A 4		1⅝"	2"	2¾"	3½"
A 2	◹	2"	2⅜"	3⅛"	3⅞"
B 4		1⅝"	2"	2¾"	3½"
B 2	◹	2"	2⅜"	3⅛"	3⅞"
C 2		2¾"	3½"	5"	6½"
C 4	◹	2	2⅜"	3⅛"	3⅞"

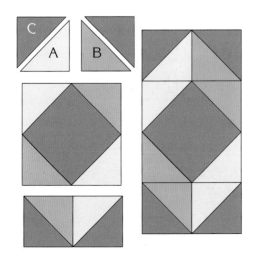

Pinwheel Block

HST—pages 12–13

Color/Cut	Subcut	4½"	6"	9"	12"
A 1		2¾"	3½"	5"	6½"
A 2	◹	2"	2⅜"	3⅛"	3⅞"
B 4		1⅝"	2"	2¾"	3½"
B 2	◹	2"	2⅜"	3⅛"	3⅞"
C 4		1⅝"	2"	2¾"	3½"

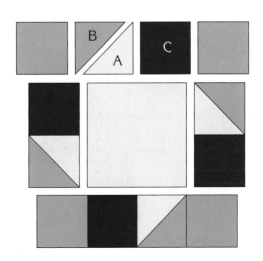

Red and White Cross

HST—pages 12–13

Color/Cut	Subcut	4½"	6"	9"	12"
A 8		2"	2⅜"	3⅛"	3⅞"
B 6		2"	2⅜"	3⅛"	3⅞"
C 2		2"	2⅜"	3⅛"	3⅞"

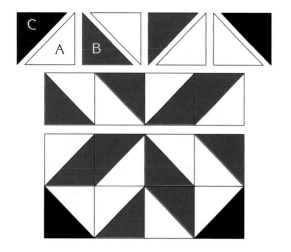

Ribbon Border

HST—pages 12–13
QST—page 14 (steps 1–4)

Color/Cut	Subcut	4½"	6"	9"	12"
A 1		3½"	4¼"	5¾"	7¼"
A 2		2"	2⅜"	3⅛"	3⅞"
B 2		2"	2⅜"	3⅛"	3⅞"
B 2		3⅛"	3⅞"	5⅜"	6⅞"

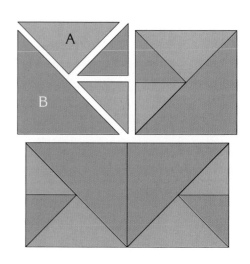

Road to Oklahoma

HST—pages 12–13

Color/Cut	Subcut	4½"	6"	9"	12"
A 6		1⅝"	2"	2¾"	3½"
A 2	◨	2"	2⅜"	3⅛"	3⅞"
B 4		1⅝"	2"	2¾"	3½"
B 2	◨	2"	2⅜"	3⅛"	3⅞"
C 2		1⅝"	2"	2¾"	3½

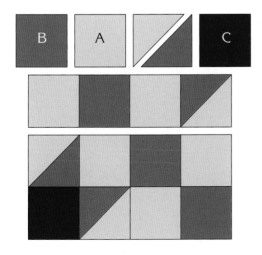

Scrap Zig Zag

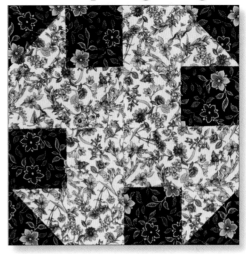

HST—pages 12–13

Color/Cut	Subcut	4½"	6"	9"	12"
A 4		1⅝" x 2¾"	2" x 3½"	2¾" x 5"	3½" x 6½"
A 2	◨	2"	2⅜"	3⅛"	3⅞"
B 4		1⅝"	2"	2¾"	3½"
B 2	◨	2"	2⅜"	3⅛"	6⅞"

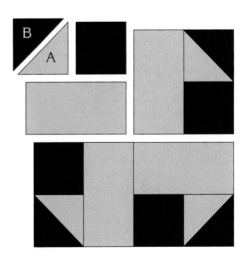

The 4 x 4 Grid Blocks

Seesaw Block

Flying Geese from Squares—page 17
Adding Corners—page 24

Color/Cut	Subcut	4½"	6"	9"	12"
*A4		1⅝"	2"	2¾"	3½"
*B 4		1⅝" x 2¾"	2" x 3½"	2¾" x 5"	3½" x 6½"
*C 4		1⅝" x 2¾"	2" x 3½"	2¾" x 5"	3½" x 6½"
*D 8		1⅝"	2"	2¾"	3½"

---TIPS---
*Use B rectangles and D squares to make
Flying Geese from Squares, page 17.

For Adding Corners, page 24,
use A squares and C rectangles.

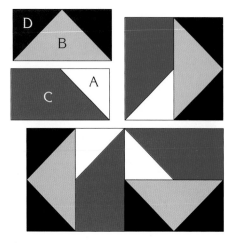

Shipping Dreams

HST—pages 12–13

Color/Cut	Subcut	4½"	6"	9"	12"
A 3		2"	2⅜"	3⅛"	3⅞"
A 2		1⅝" x 2¾"	2" x 3½"	2¾" x 5"	3½" x 6½"
B 1		1⅝" x 5"	2" x 6½"	2¾" x 9½"	3½" x 12½"
C 3		2"	2⅜"	3⅛"	3⅞"
C 2		1⅝"	2"	2¾"	3½"

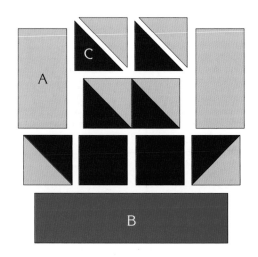

Shooting Star

HST—pages 12–13

Color/Cut	Subcut	4½"	6"	9"	12"
A 4		1⅝"	2"	2¾"	3½"
A 2	◹	2"	2⅜"	3⅛"	3⅞"
B 2	◹	2"	2⅜"	3⅛"	3⅞"
C 4	◹	2"	2⅜"	3⅛"	3⅞"
D 4		1⅝"	2"	2¾"	3½"

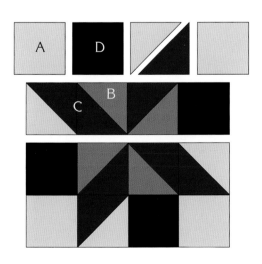

Single Sawtooth

HST—pages 12–13

Color/Cut	Subcut	4½"	6"	9"	12"
A 4		1⅝"	2"	2¾"	3½"
B 4	◹	2"	2⅜"	3⅛"	3⅞"
B 4		1⅝"	2"	2¾"	3½"
C 4	◹	2"	2⅜"	3⅛"	3⅞"

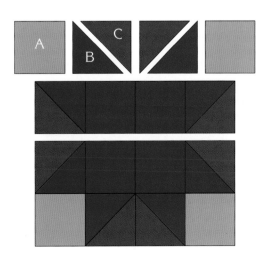

The 4 x 4 Grid Blocks

Single Star

HST—pages 12–13

Color/Cut	Subcut	4½"	6"	9"	12"
A 4		1⅝"	2"	2¾"	3½"
A 4	◰	2"	2⅜"	3⅛"	3⅞"
B 4		1⅝"	2"	2¾"	3½"
B 4	◰	2"	2⅜"	3⅛"	3⅞"

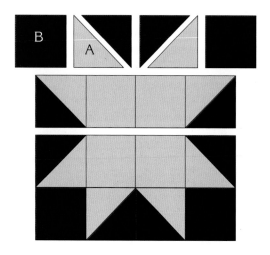

Snowflake Block

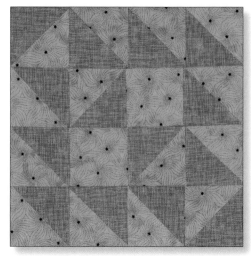

HST—pages 12–13

Color/Cut	Subcut	4½"	6"	9"	12"
A 7	◰	2"	2⅜"	3⅛"	3⅞"
A 2		1"	2"	2¾"	3½"
B 7	◰	2"	2⅜"	3⅛"	3⅞"

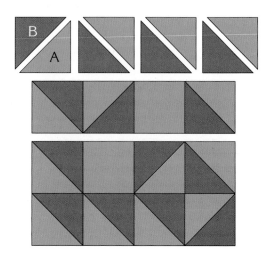

Solitaire Block

HST—pages 12–13
QST—pages 14–15

Color/Cut	Subcut	4½"	6"	9"	12"
A 2	⊠	2⅜"	2¾"	3½"	4¼"
A 4	◹	2"	2⅜"	3⅛"	3⅞"
B 4	◹	2"	2⅜"	3⅛"	3⅞"
C 2	⊠	2⅜"	2¾"	3½"	4¼"
C 2	⊠	2"	2⅜"	3⅛"	3⅞"

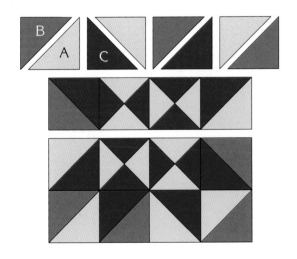

Squire Smith's Choice

HST—pages 12–13

Color/Cut	Subcut	4½"	6"	9"	12"
A 8	◹	2"	2⅜"	3⅛"	3⅞"
B 6	◹	2"	2⅜"	3⅛"	3⅞"
C 2	◹	2"	2⅜"	3⅛"	3⅞"

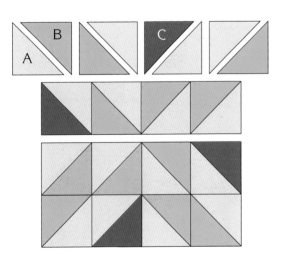

Star and Pinwheels

HST—pages 12–13
QST—page 14 (steps 1–4)

Color/Cut	Subcut	4½"	6"	9"	12"
A 6		2"	2⅜"	3⅛"	3⅞"
A 1		2⅜"	2¾"	3½"	4¼"
B 1		2⅜"	2¾"	3½"	4¼"
C 8		2"	2⅜"	3⅛"	3⅞"

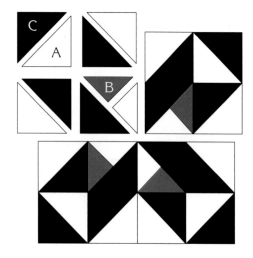

Star of Friendship

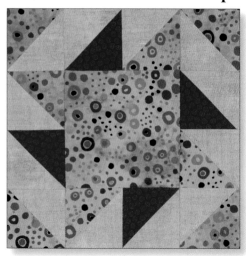

HST—pages 12–13

Color/Cut	Subcut	4½"	6"	9"	12"
A 6		2"	2⅜"	3⅛"	3⅞"
B 1		2¾"	3½"	5"	6½"
B 4		2"	2⅜"	3⅛"	3⅞"
C 2		2"	2⅜"	3⅛"	3⅞"

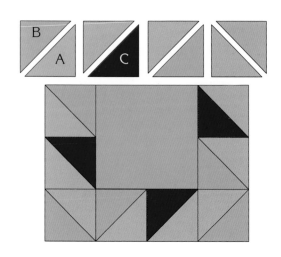

Star of the Milky Way

HST—pages 12–13

Color/Cut	Subcut		4½"	6"	9"	12"
A 8	☐	◹	2"	2⅜"	3⅛"	3⅞"
B 8	◼	◹	2"	2⅜"	3⅛"	3⅞"

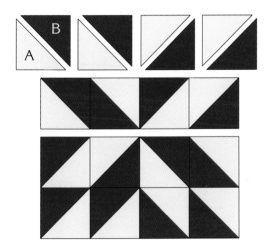

Star Puzzle Block

HST—pages 12–13
Flying Geese From Triangles —page 16

Color/Cut	Subcut		4½"	6"	9"	12"
*A 1	☐	⊠	3½"	4¼"	5¾"	7¼"
A 4	☐	◹	2	2⅜"	3⅛"	3⅞"
*B 8	◼	◹	2	2⅜"	3⅛"	3⅞"

--- TIPS ---
*Use A-QST for "geese" bodies and 8-B HSTs
for "sky" to make Flying Geese from Triangles, page 16.

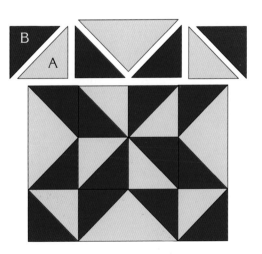

The 4 x 4 Grid Blocks

State of Louisiana

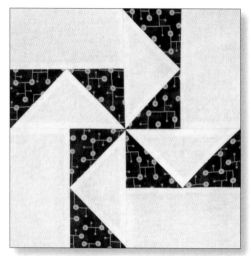

HST—pages 12–13
Flying Geese from Triangles—page 16

Color/Cut	Subcut		4½"	6"	9"	12"
A 4			1⅝" x 2¾"	2" x 3½"	2¾" x 5"	3½" x 6½"
*A 1			3½"	4¼"	5¾"	7¼"
*B 4			2"	2⅜"	3⅛"	3⅞"

—TIPS—
*Use A-QST for "geese" bodies and B-HSTs
for "sky" to make Flying Geese from Triangles page 16.

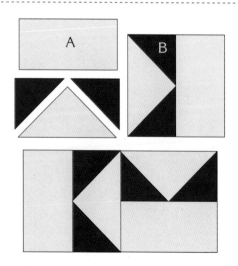

Sugar Bowl Block

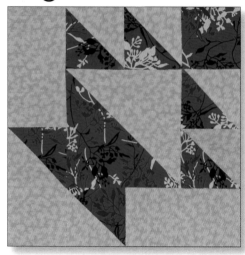

HST—pages 12–13

Color/Cut	Subcut		4½"	6"	9"	12"
A 1			3⅛"	3⅞"	5⅜"	6⅞"
A 2			1⅝" x 2¾"	2" x 3½"	2¾" x 5"	3½" x 6½"
A 1			1⅝"	2"	2¾"	3½"
A 3			2"	2⅜"	3⅛"	3⅞"
B 1			3⅛"	3⅞"	5⅜"	6⅞"
B 1			1⅝"	2"	2¾"	3½"
B 3			2"	2⅜"	3⅛"	3⅞"

—TIPS—
There will be triangles left over from B HST subcuts.

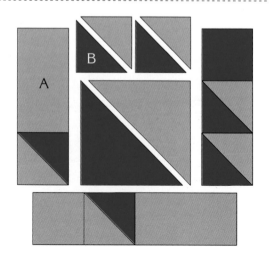

The Anvil

HST—pages 12–13

Color/Cut	Subcut	4½"	6"	9"	12"
A 4		1⅝"	2"	2¾"	3½"
A 4	�%⧄	3	2⅜"	3⅛"	3⅞"
B 4	◼⧄	3	2⅜"	3⅛"	3⅞"
C 1	◼	2¾"	3½"	5"	6½"

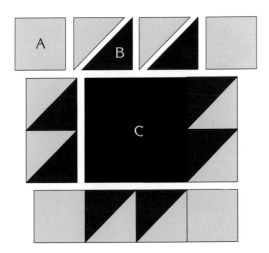

The Disk

HST—pages 12–13
Parallel Seams—page 22

Color/Cut	Subcut	4½"	6"	9"	12"
A 1	⧄	3⅛"	3⅞"	5⅜"	6⅞"
*A 2		1⅝"	2"	2¾"	3½"
B 1		1⅝"	2"	2¾"	3½"
*B 2		1⅝" x 2¾"	2" x 3½"	2¾" x 5"	3½" x 6½"
B 1	⧄	2	2⅜"	3⅛"	3⅞"
C 1	⧄	3⅛"	3⅞"	5⅜"	6⅞"
C 2		1⅝" x 2¾"	2" x 3½"	2¾" x 5"	3½" x 6½"
*C 3		1⅝"	2"	2¾"	3½"
C 1	⧄	2	2⅜"	3⅛"	3⅞"

------ TIPS ------
*B rectangles, 2-A and 2-C squares for Parallel Seams, page 22.

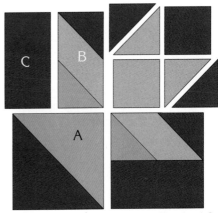

The 4 x 4 Grid Blocks

The Disk Variation

HST—pages 12–13
Adding Triangles to a Square—page 23

Color/Cut	Subcut		4½"	6"	9"	12"
A 6	☐		1⅝"	2"	2¾"	3½"
A 3	☐	◹	2"	2⅜"	3⅛"	3⅞"
B 2	◪	◹	2"	2⅜"	3⅛"	3⅞"
C 1	◪	◹	2"	2⅜"	3⅛"	3⅞"
D 1	◼	◹	3⅛"	3⅞"	5⅜"	6⅞"
E 1	◼	◹	2"	2⅜"	3⅛"	3⅞"
E 1	◼	◹	2"	2"	2¾"	3½"

TIPS
There will be a triangle left over from D HST subcut.

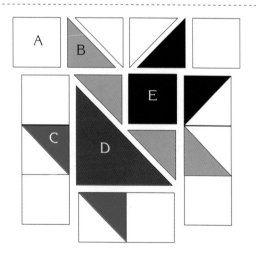

Triangle Squares

Square-in-a-Square—page 23
Four-at-a-time Flying Geese—page 18

Color/Cut	Subcut	4½"	6"	9"	12"
A 4	◻	1⅛"	2"	2¾"	3½"
*A 4	◻	2"	2⅜"	3⅛"	3⅞"
B 1	◼	2¾"	3½"	5"	6½"
*B 1	◼	3½"	4¼"	5¾"	7½"
C 4	◼	1⅛"	2"	2¾"	3½"

TIPS
*Use 4-A squares and the large B square
to make Four-at-a-Time Flying Geese, page 18.

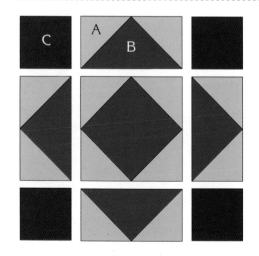

Triangle Weave

HST—pages 12–13
Adding Triangles to a Square—page 25

Color/Cut	Subcut	4½"	6"	9"	12"
A 4		1⅝"	2"	2¾"	3½"
A 5		2"	2⅜"	3⅛"	3⅞"
B 1		3½"	3⅞"	5⅜"	6⅞"
B 3		2"	2⅜"	3⅛"	3⅞"

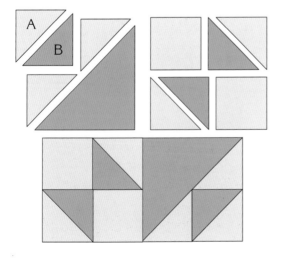

Twelve Triangles

Square-in-a-Square—page 23
Flying Geese from Squares—page 17

Color/Cut	Subcut	4½"	6"	9"	12"
A 1		2⅜"	3½"	5"	6½"
B 12		1⅝"	2"	2¾"	3½"
C 4		1⅝" x 2¾"	2" x 3½"	2¾" x 5"	3½" x 6½"

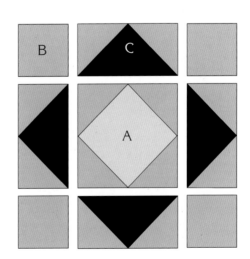

Virginia Reel

Four-at-a-time Flying Geese—page 18

Color/Cut	Subcut	4½"	6"	9"	12"
*A 1		3½"	4¼"	5¾"	7¼"
*A 4		2"	2⅜"	3⅛"	3⅞"
*B 1		3½"	4¼"	5¾"	7¼"
*B 4		2"	2⅜"	3⅛"	3⅞"

---TIPS---
*Use large A square/small B squares, and large
B square/small A squares to make
Four-at-a-Time Flying Geese, page 18.

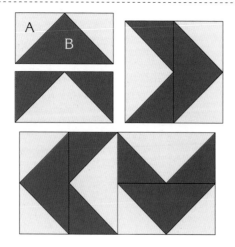

Waypoint Star

Flying Geese from Squares—page 17
Adding Corners—page 24

Color/Cut	Subcut	4½"	6"	9"	12"
*A 1		2¾"	3½"	5"	6½"
*A 3		1⅝"	2"	2¾"	3½"
*B 5		1⅝"	2"	2¾"	3½"
*B 4		1⅝" x 2¾"	2" x 3½"	2¾" x 5"	3½" x 6½"
*C 5		1⅝"	2"	2¾"	3½"

---TIPS---
*Use 3-A squares, 5-C squares, and 4-B rectangles to
make Flying Geese from Squares, page 17, and large A
square and 1-B square for Adding Corners, page 24.

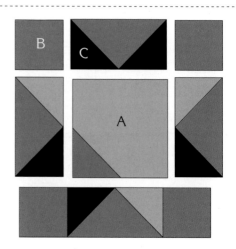

Whirligig

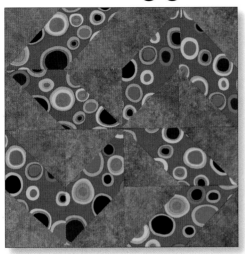

Parallel Seams—page 22

Color/Cut	Subcut	4½"	6"	9"	12"
A 16 ▩		1⅝"	2"	2¾""	3½"
B 8 ▬		1⅝" x 2¾"	2" x 3½"	2¾ x 5"	3½" x 6½"

─── TIPS ───
Virginia Reel, page 110, and Whirligig are similar. One is made with flying geese and the other with parallel seams.

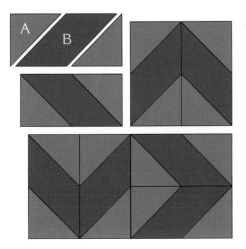

Whirlpool Block

HST—pages 12-13; Flying Geese from Squares—page 17; Square-in-a-Square—page 23
Partial Seams—page 20

Color/Cut	Subcut	4½"	6"	9"	12"
*A 12 ▢		1⅝"	2"	2¾"	3½"
A 2 ▢	◹	2"	2⅜"	3⅛"	3⅞"
B 1 ■		2¾"	3½"	5"	6½"
*B 4 ▬		1⅝" x 2¾"	2" x 3½"	2¾" x 5"	3½" x 6½"
B 2 ■	◹	2"	2⅜"	3⅛"	3⅞"

─── TIPS ───
*Use 8-A squares and 4-B rectangles to make Flying Geese from Squares, page 17.

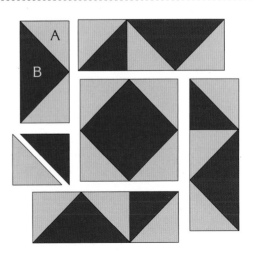

The 4 x 4 Grid Blocks

Wild Duck

HST—pages 12–13

Color/Cut	Subcut	4½"	6"	9"	12"
A 4 ▢		1⅝"	2"	2¾"	3½"
A 3 ▢	◺	2"	2⅜"	3⅛"	3⅞"
B 4 ▢		1⅝"	2"	2¾"	3½"
C 4 ▢	◺	2"	2⅜"	3⅛"	3⅞"

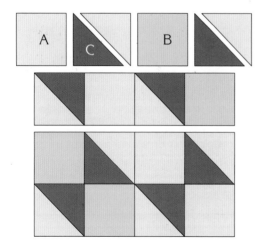

Windblown Square

*Flying Geese from Squares page 17
HST—pages 12–13; Partial Seams—page 20
Square-in-a-Square—page 23

Color/Cut	Subcut	4½"	6"	9"	12"
A 1 ▢		2¾"	3½"	5"	6½"
*A 8 ▢		1⅝"	2"	2¾"	3½"
A 2 ▢	◺	2"	2⅜"	3⅛"	3⅞"
B 2 ▢		1⅝"	2"	2¾"	3½"
B 1 ▢	◺	2"	2⅜"	3⅛"	3⅞"
*B 2 ▭		1⅝" x 2¾"	2 x 3½"	2¾" x 5"	3½" x 6½"
*C 2 ▭		1⅝" x 2¾"	2 x 3½"	2¾" x 5"	3½" x 6½"
C 2 ▭		1⅝"	2"	2¾"	3½"
C 1 ▭	◺	2"	2⅜"	3⅛"	3⅞"

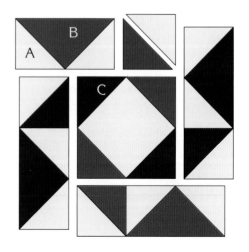

Windmill Block

HST—pages 12–13; QST—page 14 (steps 1–4); Adding Triangles to a Square—page 25

Color/Cut	Subcut	4½"	6"	9"	12"
A 4		2"	2⅜"	3⅛"	3⅞"
B 2		2"	2⅜"	3⅛"	3⅞"
B 1		3½"	4¼"	5¾"	7¼"
C 2		2"	2⅜"	3⅛"	3⅞"
D 1		3½"	4¼"	5¾"	7¼"

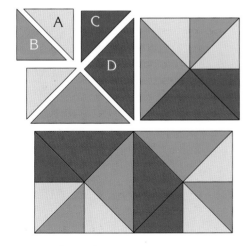

Windmill Block Variation

Four-at-a-Time Flying Geese—page 18

Color/Cut	Subcut	4½"	6"	9"	12"
A 4		1⅝"	2"	2¾"	3½"
*A 1		3½"	4¼"	5¾"	7½"
*B 4		2	2⅜"	3⅛"	3⅞"
B 4		1⅝"	2"	2¾"	3½"

TIPS

*Use 4-B squares and 1-A square to make Four-at-a-Time Flying Geese, page 18.

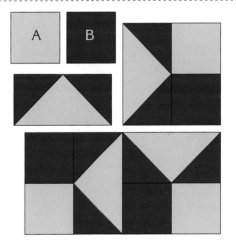

Yankee Puzzle

HST—pages 12–13; Four-at-a-Time Flying Geese—page 18; Partial Seams—page 20

Color/Cut	Subcut	4½"	6"	9"	12"
*A 4		2"	2⅜"	3⅛"	3⅞"
*A 2		2"	2⅜"	3⅛"	3⅞"
*B 1		3½"	4¼"	5¾"	7¼"
B 2	◻	2"	2⅜"	3⅛"	3⅞"
C 4	◻	2"	2⅜"	3⅛"	3⅞"

----- TIPS -----
*Use 4-A squares and 1-B square to make
Four-at-a-Time Flying Geese—page 18. Use 2-A squares
for A/C HSTs

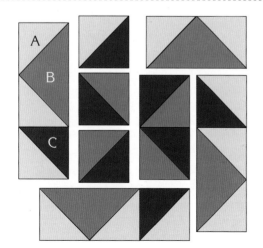

Wondering What To Do With Your Blocks?

Whether you made a lot of the same block or you made a variety, here are some ways to play around with them.

1. Organize a block swap with some quilting friends and, as a group, choose the number of blocks to exchange based on a finished project idea. Everyone makes the block design they choose. If you want the finished quilt to be coordinated, as a group, choose a colorway or a fabric collection to use. When everyone is finished making their blocks, swap away!

2. Create a Block Library. I used three ring scrapbooking binders with plastic sleeves to store my blocks. They are organized by grid size, alphabetized, and original instructions are tucked behind each block. Since the blocks have raw edges, it's a gentler way to store them without fraying.

3. Practice your quilting. I really like utility stitching. I chose a few blocks and used them to practice some utility and embroidery stitches. I made my blocks 9-inches so they are a reasonable size to handle when I stitch by hand.

4. Take a photo of a block and play around with placement and color on your computer or an app on your smart phone. Since I'm a photographer I use Photoshop. On the following page are some examples of how I manipulated blocks to make a secondary pattern. You can flip, rotate or create a mirror image. Using technology to "test" block designs is a quick, fun way to experiment and it's exciting see what happens in the process!

5. Make a quilt using one of the settings on pages 190-201. Remember that sashing helps set blocks apart from one another, making the block designs stand out. Pay attention to grid sizes if you choose not to add sashing. Blocks evenly divisible by 2 and 4 sit well together. Blocks divisible by 3 do the same. In both cases, seam lines will either line up or divide a section equally which is more pleasing to the eye.

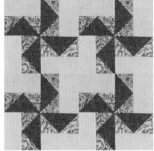

Louisiana Pinwheel
Page 37

Aunt Dinah
Page 117

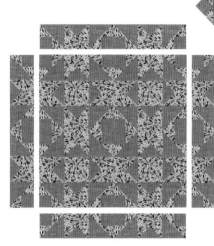

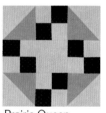
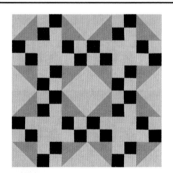

Prairie Queen
Page 127

Magnolia Block
Page 124

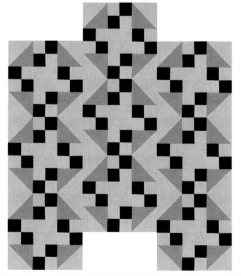

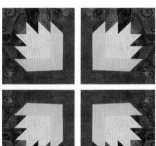

Wondering What to do with Your Blocks?

The 5 x 5 Grid Blocks

Traditional 5 x 5 grid blocks are just too pretty and interesting not to consider when designing a quilt. I looked at quite a few 4 x 4 grid blocks and tried to see how I could turn them into 5 x 5 grid blocks. I framed the Bellatrix block on page 118 on two sides. Without the frames it's a 4 x 4 grid block. As a stand alone block, it is very atypical. But if you make four and play around with turning and flipping the blocks, secondary patterns emerge that are quite surprising!

Autumn Leaf

HST—pages 12–13

Color/Cut	Subcut	5"	10"	15"
A 4	◻ ◹	1⅞"	2⅞"	3⅞"
A 4	◻	1½"	2½"	3½"
A 1	◻	2½"	4½"	6½"
A 1	▭	1½" x 2½"	2½" x 4½"	3½" x 6½"
B 4	◼ ◹	1⅞"	2⅞"	3⅞"
B 1	▬	2½" x 3½"	4½" x 6½"	6½" x 9½"
B 1	▬	1½" x 3½"	2½" x 6½"	3½" x 9½"

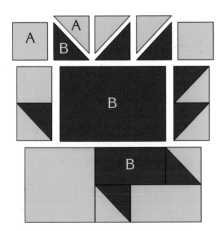

Baton Rouge Square

HST—pages 12–13
Adding Corners—page 24

Color/Cut	Subcut	5"	10"	15"
A 5	◼	1½"	2½"	3½"
A 2	◼ ◹	1⅞"	2⅞"	3⅞"
B 2	◻ ◹	1⅞"	2⅞"	3⅞"
B 4	◻	1½"	2½"	3½"
C 2	◼ ◹	1⅞"	2⅞"	3⅞"
C 4	◼	1½"	2½"	3½"
D 4	◼	1½"	2½"	3½"
D 2	◼ ◹	1⅞"	2⅞"	3⅞"

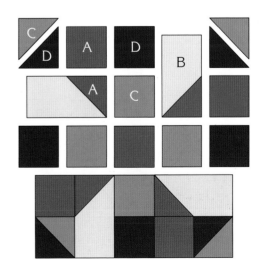

Bellatrix

HST—pages 12–13
*Four-at-a-Time Flying Geese—page 18
Designed by Sue Voegtlin

Color/Cut	Subcut	5"	10"	15"
A 1	◹	1⅞"	2⅞"	3⅞"
*A 1		3¼"	5¼"	7¼"
B 2		1½"	2½"	3½"
B 1	◹	1⅞"	2⅞"	3⅞"
B 1		1½" x 5½"	2½" x 10½"	3½" x 15½"
B		1½" x 4½"	2½" x 8½"	3½" x 12½"
*C 4	◹	1⅞"	2⅞"	3⅞"
D 1		2½"	4½"	6½"

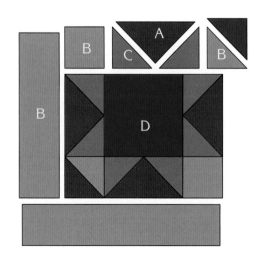

Birthday Cake

HST—pages 12–13

Color/Cut	Subcut	5"	10"	15"
A 1		1½"	2½"	3½"
A 4	◹	1⅞"	2⅞"	3⅞"
A 2		2⅞"	4⅞"	6⅞"
B 2	◹	2⅞"	4⅞"	6⅞"
C 4	◹	1⅞"	2⅞"	3⅞
C 1		2⅞"	4⅞"	6⅞"

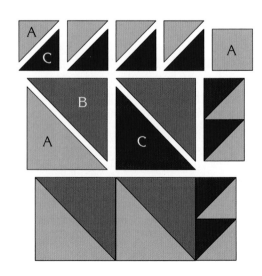

Block House

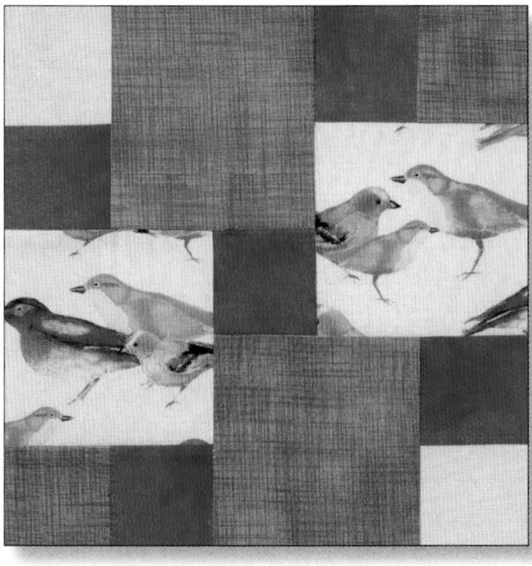

Partial Seams—page 20

Color/Cut	Subcut	5"	10"	15"
A 2		1½"	2½"	3½"
A 2		2½"	4½"	6½"
B 2		1½"	2½"	3½"
B 2		2½"	4½"	6½"
C 5		1½"	2½"	3½"

TIPS

You can try switching out the darks and lights in this block for a different look.

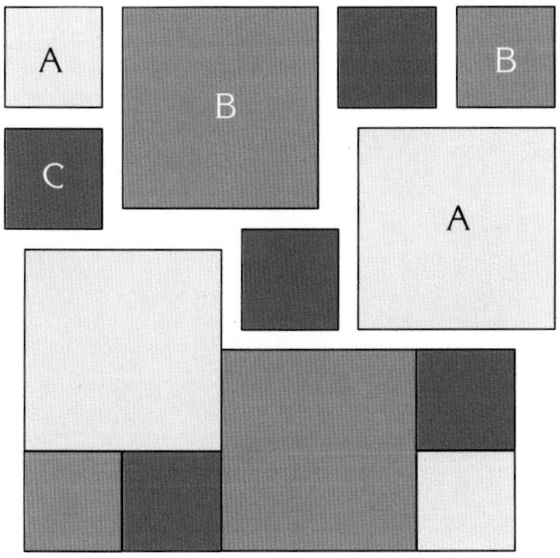

Causeways

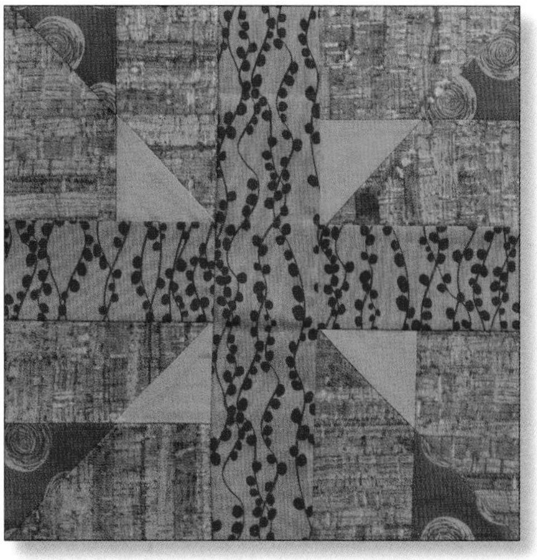

Adding Corners—24
Designed by Sue Voegtlin

Color/Cut	Subcut	5"	10"	15"
A 2		1⅞"	2⅞"	3⅞"
B 8		1½" x 2½"	2½" x 4½"	3½" x 6½"
C 9		1⅞"	2⅞"	3⅞"
D 2		1½" x 2½"	2½" x 4½"	3½" x 6½"
D 1		1½" x 5½"	2½" x 10½"	3½" x 15½"

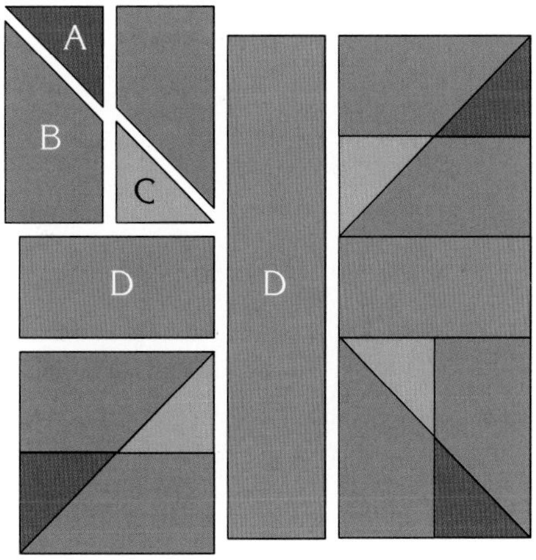

Clara's Red Cross

Add C squares to E HSTs using the "Adding Corners" technique—page 24.

Color/Cut	Subcut	5"	10"	15"
A 2 ◻ ◺		1⅞"	2⅞"	3⅞"
B 4 ◻		1⅞"	2⅞"	3⅞"
C 5 ◻		1½"	2½"	3½"
D 4 ◻		1½"	2½"	3½"
D 1 ◻		1½"	2½"	3½"
E 4 ◻		1½"	2½"	3½"
E 2 ◻ ◺		1⅞"	2⅞"	3⅞"
E 2 ◻ ◺		2⅞"	3⅞"	4⅞"

TIPS
For a different look, switch out the "B" squares with other colors. Make four blocks and see what kind of secondary patterns start to appear.

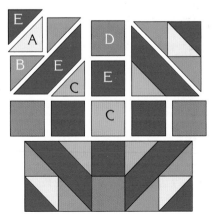

Clowns Block

Color/Cut	Subcut	5"	10"	15"
A 5 ◻ ⊠		2¼"	3¼"	4¼"
A 4 ◻		1½"	2½"	3½"
B 5 ◼ ⊠		2¼"	3¼"	4¼"
C 8 ◼		1½"	2½"	3½"
D 4 ◼		1½"	2½"	3½"

TIPS
Since there are so many seams in this block, use pins to match them up and press seams open.

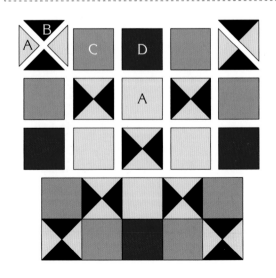

Crazy House

Adding Corners—page 24

Color/Cut	Subcut	5"	10"	15"
A 13		1½"	2½"	3½"
B 8		1½" x 2½"	2½" x 4½"	3½" x 6½"
B 4		1½"	2½"	3½"

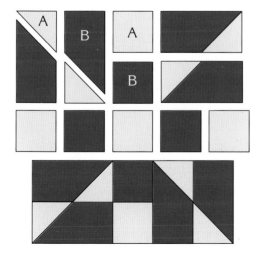

Cross Walk

HST—pages 12–13
Adding Corners—page 24
Designed by Sue Voegtlin

Color/Cut	Subcut		5"	10"	15"
A 1			1⅞"	2⅞"	3⅞"
A 11			1½"	2½"	3½"
A 2			1½" x 2½"	2½" x4½"	3½" x 6½"
B 4			1½"	2½"	3½"
B 2			1½" x 3½"	2½" x 6½"	3½" x 9½"
C 1			1½" x 5½"	2½" x 10½"	3½" x15½"
C 1			1½" x 2½"	2½" x 4½"	3½" x 6½"
C 2			1½"	2½"	3½"
C 1			1⅞"	2⅞"	3⅞"

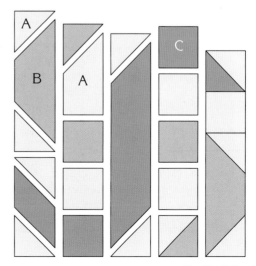

The 5 x 5 Grid Blocks

Corvid's Curiosity

HST—pages 12–13

Color/Cut	Subcut	5"	10"	15"
A 2 ⬛		1½" x 5½"	2½" x 10½"	3½" x15½"
A 2 ⬛		1½" x 3½"	2½" x 6½"	3½" x 9½"
A 2 ◪	◹	1⅞"	2⅞"	3⅞"
B 4 ◪		1½"	2½"	3½
B 2 ◻	◹	1⅞"	2⅞"	3⅞"
B 1 ◪		1½"	2½"	3½

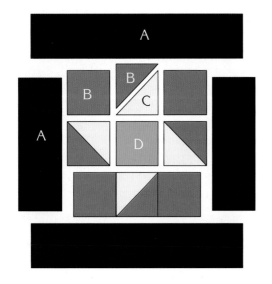

Delectable Mountain

HST—pages 12–13

Color/Cut	Subcut	5"	10"	15"
A 1 ◻		3⅞"	6⅞"	9⅞"
A 4 ◻	◹	1⅞"	2⅞"	3⅞"
B 1 ◪		1½"	2½"	3½
B 3 ◪	◺	1⅞"	2⅞"	3⅞"
B 1 ◪	◺	5⅞"	10⅞"	15⅞"

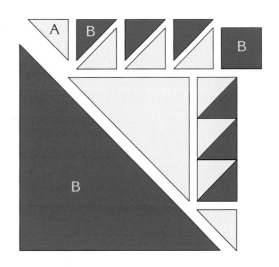

Diamond Panes

HST—pages 12–13

Color/Cut	Subcut	5"	10"	15"
A 2		2⅞"	4⅞"	6⅞"
A 2		1½" x 2½"	2½" x 4½"	3½" x 6½"
B 2		2⅞"	4⅞"	6⅞"
B 1		1½" x 5½"	2½" x 10½"	3½" x 15½"

─── TIPS ───
Pay attention to orientation of HSTs.

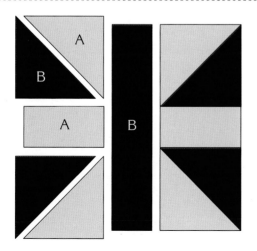

Double Baskets

Flying Geese from Squares—page 17
Adding Corners—page 24

Color/Cut	Subcut	5"	10"	15"
A 2		2⅞"	4⅞"	6⅞"
A 3		1⅞"	2⅞"	3⅞"
A 7		1½"	2½"	3½"
B 2		2⅞"	4⅞"	6⅞"
B 3		1⅞"	2⅞"	3⅞"
B 1		1½" x 2½"	2½" x 4½"	3½" x 6½"

─── TIPS ───
Pay attention to orientation of HSTs.

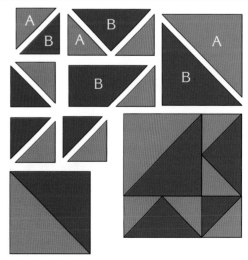

Farmer's Daughter

Color/Cut	Subcut	5"	10"	15"
A 4		1½" x 3½"	2½" x 6½"	3½" x 9½"
B 4		1½"	2½"	3½"
C 5		1½"	2½"	3½"
D 12		1½"	2½"	3½"

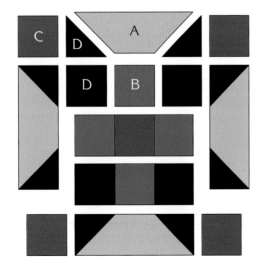

Flying Squares

Partial Seams—page 20

Color/Cut	Subcut	5"	10"	15"
A 4		1½"	2½"	3½"
B 5		1½"	2½"	3½"
C 4		1½"	2½"	3½"
D 4		1½" x 3½"	2½" x 6½"	3½" x 9½"

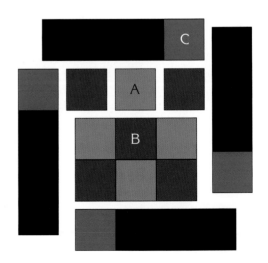

Fool's Square

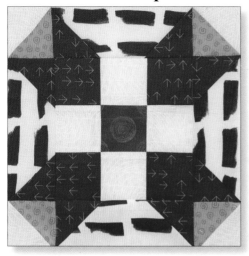

HST—pages 12–13
Adding Corners—page 24

Color/Cut	Subcut	5"	10"	15"
A 4	☐	1½"	2½"	3½"
A 2	◿	1⅞"	2⅞"	3⅞"
B 4	▭	1½" x 3½"	2½" x 6½"	3½" x 9½"
C 2	◿	1⅞"	2⅞"	3⅞"
D 13	■	1½"	2½"	3½"

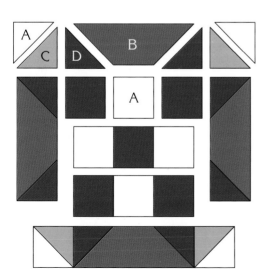

Grandmother's Choice

Adding Triangles to a Square—page 25

Color/Cut	Subcut	5"	10"	15"
A 2	◿	2⅞"	4⅞"	6⅞"
A 5	☐	1½"	2½"	3½"
B 4	◿	1⅞"	2⅞"	3⅞"
B 4	▭	1½" x 2½"	2½" x 4½"	3½" x 6½"

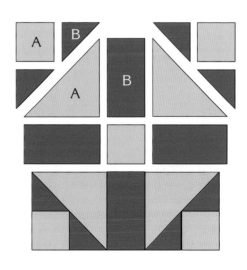

Greek Cross

Adding Corners—page 24

Color/Cut	Subcut	5"	10"	15"
A 6		1½"	2½"	3½"
A 5		1½" x 3½"	2½" x 6½"	3½" x 9½"
B 4		1½"	2½"	3½"
C 8		1½"	2½"	3½"

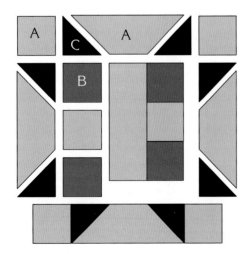

Jen's Little Jewel

Flying Geese from Squares—page 17
Designed by Sue Voegtlin

Color/Cut	Subcut	5"	10"	15"
A 6	◸	1⅞"	2⅞"	3⅞"
A 8		1½"	2½"	3½"
B 6	◸	1⅞"	2⅞"	3⅞"
B 5		1½"	2½"	3½"

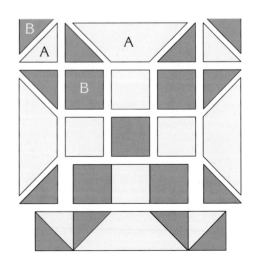

Loess Hills

HST—pages 12–13
QST—pages 14–15
Designed by Sue Voegtlin

Color/Cut	Subcut	5"	10"	15"
A 2	▭	1½" x 5½"	2½" x 10½"	3½" x 15½"
A 2	◻ ⧄	1⅞"	2⅞"	3⅞"
A 3	◻ ⊠	2¼"	3¼"	4¼"
B 8	◻ ⧄	1⅞"	2⅞"	3⅞"
B 1	◻ ⊠	2¼"	3¼"	4¼"
C 3	◼ ⊠	2¼"	3¼"	4¼"

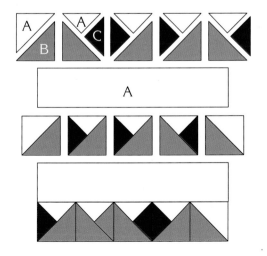

Love, Almost

Adding Corners—page 24
Designed by Sue Voegtlin

Color/Cut	Subcut	5"	10"	15"
A 1	▭	1½" x 4½"	2½" x 8½"	3½" x 12½"
A 1	▭	1½" x 3½"	2½" x 6½"	3½" x 9½"
A 1	▭	1½" x 2½"	2½" x 4½"	3½" x 6½"
A 1	◻	1½"	2½"	3½"
B 2	▭	1½" x 4½"	2½" x 8½"	3½" x 12½"
B 2	▭	1½" x 2½"	2½" x 4½"	3½" x 6½"
C 7	◼	1½"	2½"	3½"

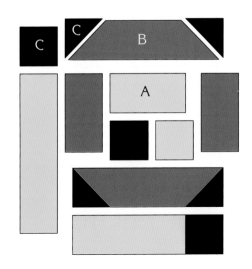

Mrs. Anderson's Quilt

Adding Corners—page 24

Color/Cut	Subcut	5"	10"	15"
A 20		1½"	2½"	3½"
B 4		2½"	4½"	6½"
B 5		1½"	2½"	3½"

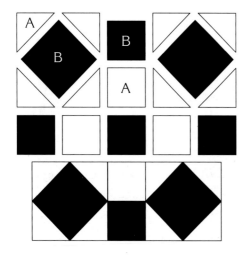

Mrs. Keller's Nine-Patch

HST—page 12–13
Adding Corners—page 24

Color/Cut	Subcut	5"	10"	15"
A 4		1½" x 3½"	2½" x 6½"	3½" x 9½"
A 5		1½"	2½"	3½"
A 2		1⅞"	2⅞"	3⅞"
*B 12		1½"	2½"	3½"
B 2		1⅞"	2⅞"	3⅞"

-----TIPS-----
*Use 8-B squares to add corners to rectangles.

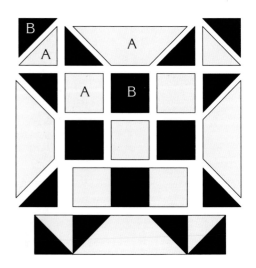

New Domino

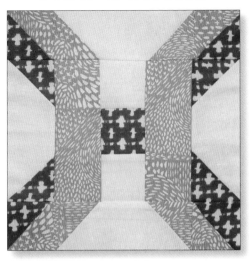

Adding Corners—page 24

Color/Cut	Subcut	5"	10"	15"
A 2		1⅞"	2⅞"	3⅞"
A 4		1½"	2½"	3½"
A 2		1½" x 3½"	2½" x 6½"	3½" x 9½"
B 4		1½" x 3½"	2½" x 6½"	3½" x 9½"
B 2		1½"	2½"	3½"
C 2		1⅞"	2⅞"	3⅞"
C 5		1½"	2½"	3½"

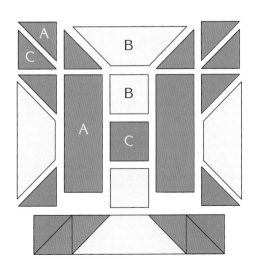

Oregon Block

HST—pages 12–13
Adding Corners —page 24

Color/Cut	Subcut	5"	10"	15"
A 4		1½" x 3½"	2½" x 6½"	3½" x 9½"
A 4		1½"	2½"	3½"
B 2		1⅞"	2⅞"	3⅞"
B 4		1½"	2½"	3½"
C 2		1⅞"	2⅞"	3⅞"
CC4		1½"	2½"	3½"
D 4		1½"	2½"	3½"
E 1		1½"	2½"	3½"

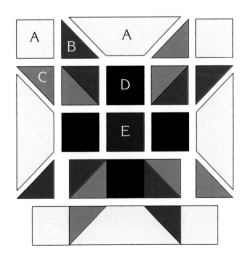

The 5 x 5 Grid Blocks

Pines Block

HST—pages 12–13
Designed by Sue Voegtlin

Color/Cut	Subcut	5"	10"	15"
A 2		1½"	2½"	3½"
A 2	◻	1⅞"	2⅞"	3⅞"
B 4	◻	1⅞"	2⅞"	3⅞"
C 4	◻	1⅞"	2⅞"	3⅞"
D 3	◻	1⅞"	2⅞"	3⅞"
E 1	◻	1⅞"	2⅞"	3⅞"
F 1		1½" x 5½"	2½" x 10½"	3½" x 15½"
F 1		1½" x 4½"	2½" x 8½"	3½" x 12½"

> **TIPS**
> Because there are so many seams,
> press them open so the block lays flat.

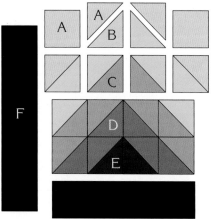

Propeller Block

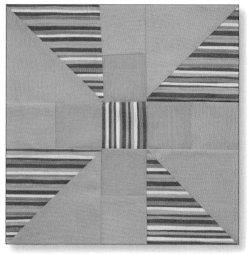

HST—pages 12–13

Color/Cut	Subcut	5"	10"	15"
A 4		1½"	2½"	3½"
A 2	◻	2⅞"	4⅞"	6⅞"
B 4		1½"	2½"	3½"
C 2	◻	2⅞"	4⅞"	6⅞"
C 1		1½"	2½"	3½"

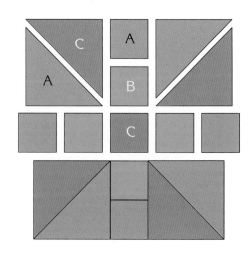

Red Cross #1

Color/Cut	Subcut	5"	10"	15"
A 6	■	1½"	2½"	3½"
A 1	▬	1½" x 3½"	2½" x 6½"	3½" x 9½"
B 4	■	1½"	2½"	3½"
B 4	▬	1½" x 3½"	2½" x 6½"	3½" x 9½"

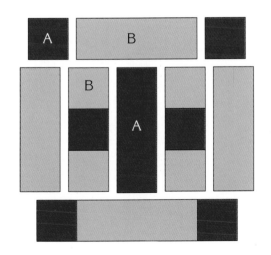

Sister's Choice

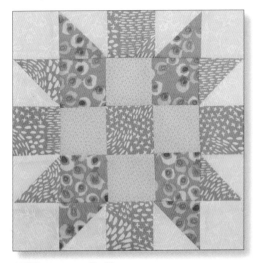

HST—pages 12-13

Color/Cut	Subcut	5"	10"	15"
A 4	☐		1½"	2½"	3½"
A 4	☐ ◺	1⅞"	2⅞"	3⅞"
B 4	■	1½"	2½"	3½"
C 5	■	1½"	2½"	3½"
C 2	■ ◹	1⅞"	2⅞"	3⅞"
D 2	■ ◹	1⅞"	2⅞"	3⅞"
D 4	■	1½"	2½"	3½"

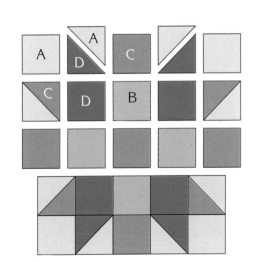

Split Square

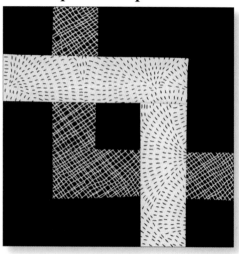

Designed by Sue Voegtlin

Color/Cut	Subcut	5"	10"	15"
A 1		1½" x 3½"	2½" x 6½"	3½" x 9½"
A 1		1½" x 4½"	2½" x 8½"	3½" x12½"
B 3		1½"	2½"	3½"
B 1		1½" x 2½"	2½" x 4½"	3½" x6½"
C 5		1½"	2½"	3½"
C 2		1½" x 3½"	2½" x 6½"	3½" x 9½"
C 1		1½" x 2½"	2½" x 4½"	3½" x6½"

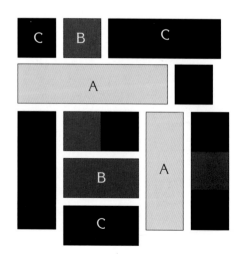

Spool Block

HST—pages 12–13
Adding Corners—page 24

Color/Cut	Subcut	5"	10"	15"
A 4		1½"	2½"	3½"
A 2		1½" x 3½"	2½" x 6½"	3½" x 9½"
B 1		3½"	6½"	9½"
C 2		1½" x5½"	2½" x 10½"	3½" x15½"

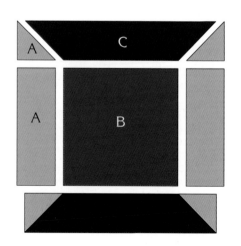

Two Pair

HST—pages 12–13
Designed by Sue Voegtlin

Color/Cut	Subcut	5"	10"	15"
A 4		1⅞"	2⅞"	3⅞"
A 2		2½"	4½"	6½"
A 5		1½"	2½"	3½"
B 2		1⅞"	2⅞"	3⅞"
B 2		1½"	2½"	3½"
C 2		1½"	2½"	3½"
C 2		1⅞"	2⅞"	3⅞"

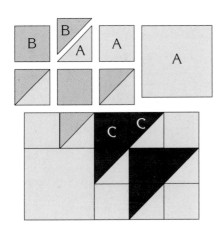

Water Trough

Designed by Sue Voegtlin

Color/Cut	Subcut	5"	10"	15"
A 4		1½"	2½"	3½"
B 6		1½"	2½"	3½"
B 1		1½" x 3½"	2½" x 6½"	3½" x 9½"
C 2		1½"	2½"	3½"
C 2		1½" x 5½"	2½" x 10½"	3½" x 15½"

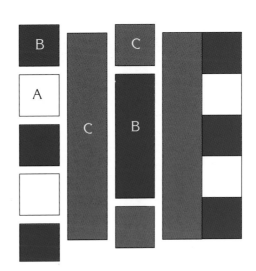

Wheel of Fortune

HST—pages 12–13

Color/Cut		Subcut	5"	10"	15"
A 8		◻	1⅞"	2⅞"	3⅞"
B 8		◻	1⅞"	2⅞"	3⅞"
C 2			1½" x 2½"	2½" x 4½"	3½" x 6½"
C 1			1½" x 5½"	2½" x 10½"	3½" x 15½"

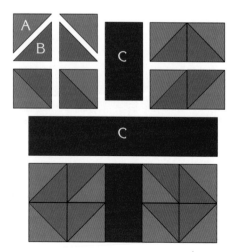

Whirling Square

HST—pages 12–13

Color/Cut		Subcut	5"	10"	15"
A 4			1½" x 3½"	2½" x 6½"	3½" x 9½"
A 4			1½"	2½"	3½"
B 4		◻	1⅞"	2⅞"	3⅞"
C 1			1½"	2½"	3½"
D 4		◻	1⅞"	2⅞"	3⅞"

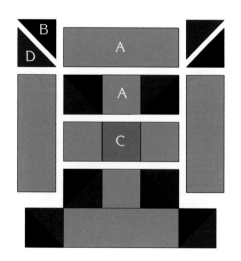

Winter to Spring

HST—pages 12–13
Designed by Sue Voegtlin

Color/Cut	Subcut	5"	10"	15"
A 4	◻ ◹	1⅞"	2⅞"	3⅞"
B 5	◻	1⅞"	2⅞"	3⅞"
C 4	◻ ◹	1½"	2½"	3½"
C 12	◼	1½"	2½"	3½"

---TIPS---
Pay attention to orientation of HSTs.

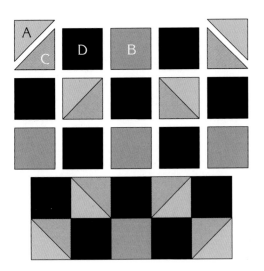

Wishing Ring

HST—pages 12–13

Color/Cut	Subcut	5"	10"	15"
A 4	◻ ◹	1⅞"	2⅞"	3⅞"
B 4	◻ ◹	1⅞"	2⅞"	3⅞"
C 5	◻	1½"	2½"	3½"
D 12	◼	1½"	2½"	3½"

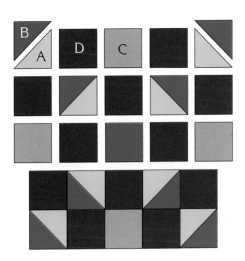

The 6 x 6 Grid Blocks

When it came time to make 6 x 6 grid blocks, I was a bit apprehensive. The pieces were smaller and the number of parts within the block increased dramatically. But I loved the detail that started to appear as more pieces were added to the block. Since the pieces were smaller, it was a great way to use up my little scraps that seemed too small to save. It turns out, these blocks became my favorite to make.

Aunt Dinah

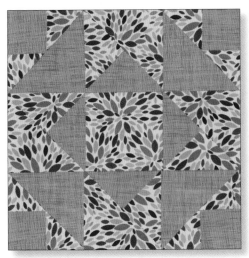

HST—pages 12–13; QST—page 14 (steps 1–4)
Adding Triangles to a Square—page 25

Color/Cut		Subcut	4½"	6"	9"	12"
A 2		◹	2⅜"	2⅞"	3⅞"	4⅞"
A 4		◹	1⅝"	1⅞"	2⅜"	2⅞"
A 1		⊠	2¾"	3¼"	4¼"	5¼"
A 1			2"	2½"	3½"	4½"
B 1		⊠	2¾"	3¼"	4¼"	5¼"
B 4			1¼"	1½"	2"	2½"
B 2		◹	2⅜"	2⅞"	3⅞"	4⅞"

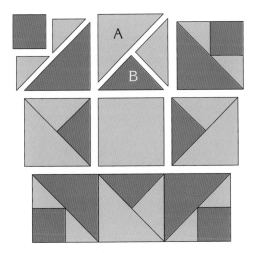

Aunt Sukey's Choice

Flying Geese from Squares—page 17

Color/Cut		Subcut	4½"	6"	9"	12"
*A 12			1¼"	1½"	2"	2½"
*A 8			1¼" x 2"	1½" x 2½"	2" x 3½"	2½" x 4½"
*B 12			1¼"	1½"	2"	2½"
*B 4			1¼" x 2"	1½" x 2½"	2" x 3½"	2½" x 4½"
C 1			2"	2½"	3½"	4½"

---TIPS---
*Use 8-A squares/4-B rectangles and 8-B squares/4-A
rectangles to make Flying Geese from Squares on page 17.

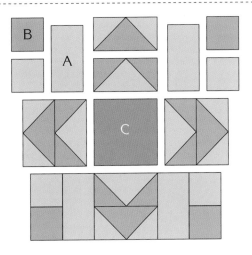

Bowl of Fruit

HST—pages 12–13

Color/Cut	Subcut	4½"	6"	9"	12"
A 2		2"	2½"	3½"	4½"
A 1		2⅜"	2⅞"	3⅞"	4⅞"
B 3		1¼"	1½"	2"	2½"
B 1		2⅜"	2⅞"	3⅞"	4⅞"
C 21		1¼"	1½"	2"	2½"
	assorted colors				

TIPS
There will be triangles left over from A & B HST subcuts.

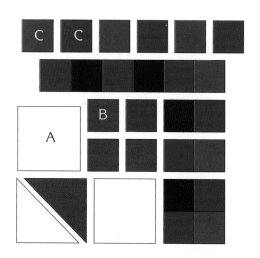

Building Blocks

Adding Corners—page 24
Parallel Seams—page 22

Color/Cut	Subcut	4½"	6"	9"	12"
A 4		2"	2½"	3½"	4½"
*A 8		1¼"	1½"	2"	2½"
*B 4		1¼" x 2¾"	1½" x 3½"	2" x 5"	2½" x 6½"
*C 4		1¼"	1½"	2"	2½"
*C 4		1¼" x 2"	1½" x 2½"	2" x 3½"	2½" x 4½"

TIPS
*Use 4-B rectangles, 4-A, 4-C squares, to make Parallel
Seams on page 22. For Adding Corners on page 24.
Use 4-C rectangles and 4-A squares.

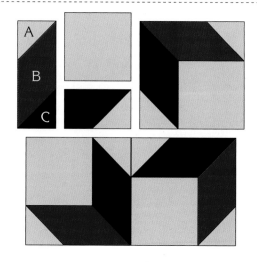

Children's Delight

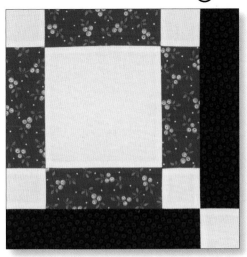

Color/Cut	Subcut	4½"	6"	9"	12"
A 1	☐	2¾"	3½"	5"	6½"
A 5	☐	1¼"	1½"	2"	2½"
B 4	▬	1¼" x 2¾"	1½" x 3½"	2" x 5"	2½" x 6½"
C 2	▬	1¼" x 4¼"	1½" x 5½"	2" x 8½"	2½" x 11½"

─── TIPS ───
You can try switching out the darks
and lights in this block for a different look.

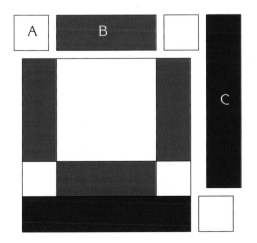

Crossword Block

Color/Cut	Subcut	4½"	6"	9"	12"
A 8	☐	1¼" x 2"	1½" x 2½"	2" x 3½"	2½" x 4½"
A 10	☐	1¼"	1½"	2"	2½"
B 10	■	1¼"	1½"	2"	2½"

─── TIPS ───
For a different look, switch out the "B" squares
with other colors. Make four blocks and see what
kind of secondary patterns start to appear.

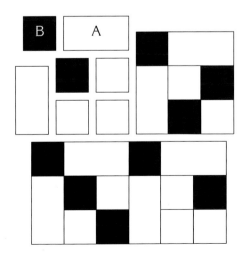

Domino Block (light)

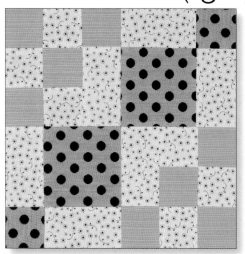

Color/Cut	Subcut	4½"	6"	9"	12"
A 6		1¼" x 2"	1½" x 2½"	2" x 3½"	2½" x 4½"
A 6		1¼"	1½"	2"	2½"
B 8		1¼"	1½"	2"	2½"
C 2		2"	2½"	3½"	4½"
C 2		1¼"	1½"	2"	2½"

---TIPS---
Since there are so many seams in this block,
use pins to match them up.

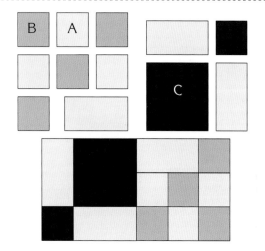

Domino Block (dark)

Color/Cut	Subcut	4½"	6"	9"	12"
A 8		1¼"	1½"	2"	2½"
B 2		2"	2½"	3½"	4½"
B 2		1¼"	1½"	2"	2½"
C 6		1¼"	1½"	2"	2½"
C 2		1¼" x 2"	1½" x 2½"	2" x 3½"	2½" x 4½"
D 4		1¼" x 2"	1½" x 2½"	2" x 3½"	2½" x 4½"

---TIPS---
It's interesting to see how color can change the look
of the Domino block, switching from lights to darks.

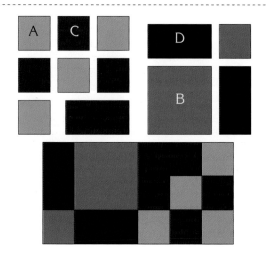

Flagstones Block

Adding Corners—page 24

Color/Cut	Subcut	4½"	6"	9"	12"
A 10		1¼"	1½"	2"	2½"
*A 2		2¾"	3½"	5"	6½"
*B 16		1¼"	1½"	2"	2½"

─────── TIPS ───────
*For Adding Corners, page 24,
use 2 large A squares and 8-B squares.

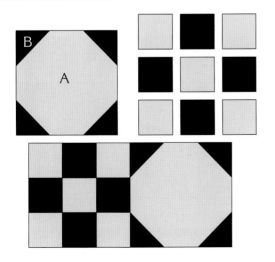

Flying Darts Block

QST—page 15
Flying Geese from Squares—page 17

Color/Cut	Subcut	4½"	6"	9"	12"
A 4		1¼" x 2¾"	1½" x 3½"	2" x 5"	2½" x 6½"
*A 2		1¼" x 2"	1½" x 2½"	2" x 3½"	2½" x 4½"
A 2	⊠	2¾"	3¼"	4¼"	5¼"
*A 4		1¼"	1½"	2"	2½"
*B 2		1¼" x 2"	1½" x 2½"	2" x 3½"	2½" x 4½"
B 2	⊠	2¾"	3¼"	4¼"	5¼"
*B 4		1¼"	1½"	2"	2½"

─────── TIPS ───────
*Use 2-A rectangles/4-B squares, and 2-B rectangles/4-A
squares to make Flying Geese from Squares on page 17.

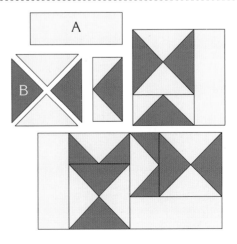

Four Crowns

HST—pages 12–13
*Flying Geese from Squares—page 17
Adding Triangles to a Square—page 23

Color/Cut		Subcut	4½"	6"	9"	12"
A 4		◤	1⅝"	1⅞"	2⅜""	2⅞"
*A 8			1¼"	1½"	2"	2½"
*A 4			1¼" x 2"	1½" x 2½"	2" x 3½"	2½" x 4½"
*B 4			1¼" x 2"	1½" x 2½"	2" x 3½"	2½" x 4½"
B 2		◥	2⅜"	2⅞"	3⅞"	4⅞"
*B 8			1¼"	1½"	2"	2½"
C 1			2"	2½"	3½"	4½"
C 4			1¼"	1½"	2"	2½"

> ──── TIPS ────
> *Use 8-A squares/4-B rectangles and 8-B squares/4-A
> rectangles to make Flying Geese from Squares on page 17.

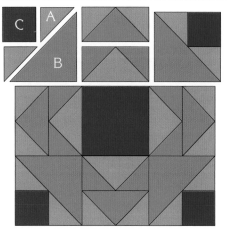

Framed Squares

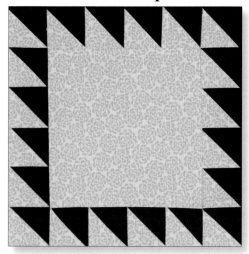

HST—pages 12–13
Pay attention to orientation of HSTs.

Color/Cut		Subcut	4½"	6"	9"	12"
A 1			3½"	4½"	6½"	8½"
A 10		◹	1⅝"	1⅞"	2⅜"	2⅞"
B 10		◹	1⅝"	1⅞"	2⅜"	2⅞"

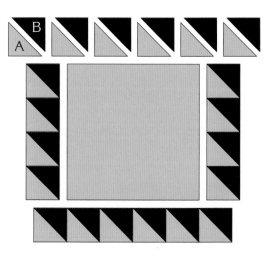

Hour Glass

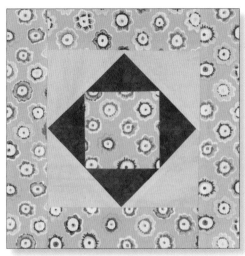

HST—pages 12–13
Square-in-a-Square—page 25

Color/Cut	Subcut	4½"	6"	9"	12"
A 2		2⅜"	2⅞"	3⅞"	4⅞"
B 1		2"	2½"	3½"	4½"
B 2		1¼" x 3½"	1½" x 4½"	2" x 6½"	2½" x 8½"
B 2		1¼" x 5"	1½" x 6½"	2" x 9½"	2½" x 12½"
C 2		1⅞"	2-1/4"	3"	3⅝"

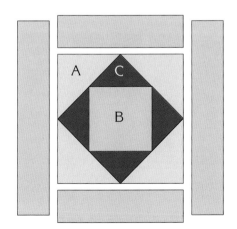

Jacob's Ladder

HST—pages 12–13

Color/Cut	Subcut	4½"	6"	9"	12"
A 2	◹	2⅜"	2⅞"	3⅞"	4⅞"
A 10		1¼"	1½"	2"	2½"
B 2	◹	2⅜"	2⅞"	3⅞"	4⅞"
B 10		1¼"	1½"	2"	2½"

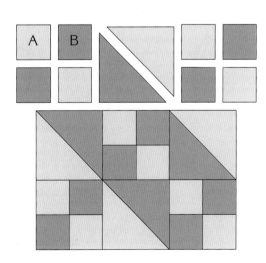

Lady of the Lake

HST—pages 12–13

Color/Cut		Subcut	4½"	6"	9"	12"
A 1			3⅞"	4⅞"	6⅞"	8⅞"
A 10			1⅝"	1⅞"	2⅜"	2⅞"
B 1			3⅞"	4⅞"	6⅞"	8⅞"
B 10			1⅜"	1⅝"	2⅜"	2⅞"

TIPS
There will be triangles left over from A and B HST subcuts.

Magnolia Block

TIPS
*For Adding Corners on page 24,
use squares and rectangles.

Color/Cut		Subcut	4½"	6"	9"	12"
A 1			2"	2½"	3½"	4½"
*A 4			1¼"	1½"	2"	2½"
*B 2			1¼"	1½"	2"	2½"
B 1			1¼" x 2"	1½" x 2½"	2" x 3½"	2½" x 4½"
B 1			1¼" x 2¾"	1½" x 3½"	2" x 5"	2½" x 6½"
*C 6			1¼" x 2"	1½" x 2½"	2" x 3½"	2½" x 4½"
C 1			2"	2½"	3½"	4½"
*C 2			1¼"	1½"	2"	2½2"
*D 1			1¼" x 4¼"	1½" x 5½"	2" x 8"	2½" x 10½"
*D 1			1¼" x 5	1½" x 6½"	2" x 9½"	2½" x 12½"

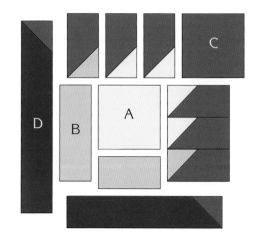

Maple Leaf Block

HST—pages 12–13

Color/Cut	Subcut	4½"	6"	9"	12"
A 2		2¾"	3½"	5"	6½"
A 4	◹	1⅝"	1⅞"	2⅜"	2⅞"
A 2		1¼"	1½"	2"	2½"
B 2		2"	2½"	3½"	4½"
B 4	◹	1⅝"	1⅞"	2⅜"	2⅞"

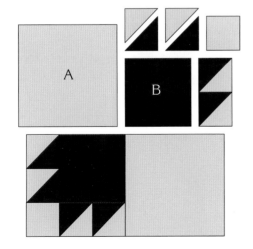

Maple Leaf Variation

Flying Geese from Squares—page 17

Color/Cut	Subcut	4½"	6"	9"	12"
A 4		1¼" x 2"	1½" x 2½"	2" x 3½"	2½" x 4½"
B 1		2"	2½"	3½"	4½"
*B 12		1¼"	1½"	2"	2½"
*C 8		1¼" x 2"	1½" x 2½"	2" x 3½"	2½" x 4½"
C 4		1¼"	1½"	2"	2½"

------TIPS------
*Use 8-B squares and 4-C rectangles to make
Flying Geese from Squares on page 17.

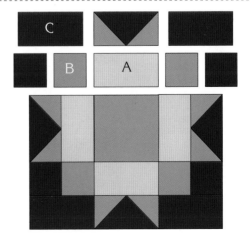

Old Crow

HST—pages 12–13

Color/Cut	Subcut	4½"	6"	9"	12"
A 2 ⬜		2"	2½"	3½"	4½"
A 8 ⬜	◺	1⅝"	1⅞"	2⅜"	2⅞"
A 2 ⬜		1¼"	1½"	2"	2½"
B 2 ⬛		2"	2½"	3½"	4½"
B 8 ⬛	◺	1⅝"	1⅞"	2⅜"	2⅞"
B 2 ⬛		1¼"	1½"	2"	2½"

------ TIPS ------
Pay attention orientation of HSTs.

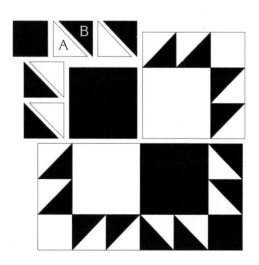

Ozark Maple Leaf

HST—pages 12–13

Color/Cut	Subcut	4½"	6"	9"	12"
A 2		2"	2½"	3½"	4½"
A 4		1¼"	1½"	2"	2½"
A 4	◹	1⅝"	1⅞"	2⅜"	2⅞"
B 6		1¼"	1½"	2"	2½"
B 4	◹	1⅝"	1⅞"	2⅜"	2⅞"
B 2		1¼" x 2"	1½" x 2½"	2" x 3½"	2½" x 4½"
B 2		1¼" x 2¾"	1½" x 3½"	2" x 5"	2½" x 6½"

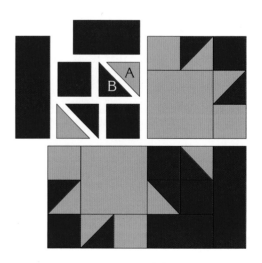

Prairie Queen

HST—pages 12–13

Color/Cut		Subcut	4½"	6"	9"	12"
A 2		◳	2⅜"	2⅞"	3⅞"	4⅞"
A 8			1¼"	1½"	2"	2½"
A 1			2"	2½"	3½"	4½"
B 2		◳	2⅜"	2⅞"	3⅞"	4⅞"
C 8			1¼"	1½"	2"	2½"

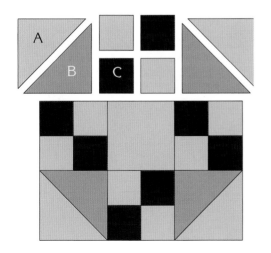

Pudding and Pie

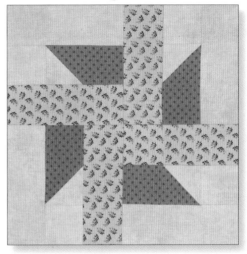

Adding Corners—page 24

Color/Cut		Subcut	4½"	6"	9"	12"
A 4			1¼" x 2¾"	1½" x 3½"	2" x 5"	2½" x 6½"
*A 8			1¼"	1½"	2"	2½"
B 4			1¼" x 2¾"	1½" x 3½"	2" x 5"	2½" x 6½"
*C 4			1¼" x 2"	1½" x 2½"	2" x 3½"	2½" x 4½"

-----TIPS-----
*For Adding Corners, use 4-A squares and C rectangles.

The four segments of this block are identical;
they are simply turned to make the pattern.

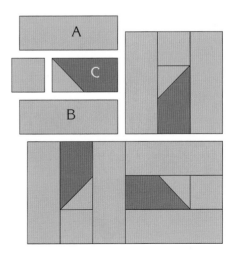

Quatrefoil Block

Adding Corners—page 24

Color/Cut	Subcut	4½"	6"	9"	12"
A 1		2"	2½"	3½"	4½"
*A 16		1¼"	1½"	2"	2½"
B 4		1¼"	1½"	2"	2½"
*C 4		2"	2½"	3½"	4½"
C 4		1¼"	1½"	2"	2½"

─────TIPS─────
*For Adding Corners, page 24, use B, C, & D squares.

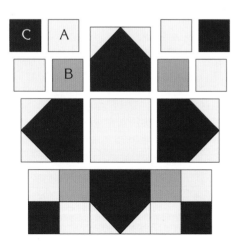

Queen's Favorite

Square-in-a-Square—page 23
Adding Corners—page 24

Color/Cut	Subcut	4½"	6"	9"	12"
A 1		2"	2½"	3½"	4½"
*B 20		1¼"	1½"	2"	2½"
*C 8		2"	2½"	3½"	4½"
*D 16		1¼"	1½"	2"	2½"

─────TIPS─────
*For Adding Corners, page 24, use B, C, & D squares.

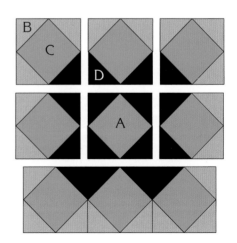

Red Cross #2

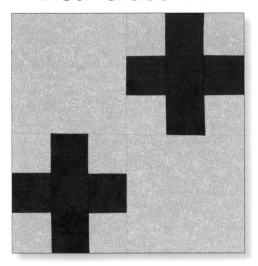

Color/Cut	Subcut	4½"	6"	9"	12"
A 2		2¾"	3½"	5"	6½"
A 8		1¼"	1½"	2"	2½"
B 2		1¼" x 2¾"	1½" x 3½"	2" x 5"	2½" x 6½"
B 4		1¼"	1½"	2"	2½"

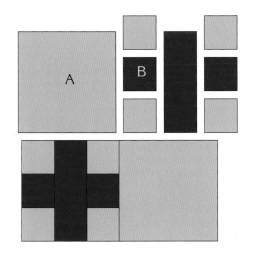

Summer Winds

HST—pages 12–13
Adding Triangles to a Square —page 25

Color/Cut	Subcut	4½"	6"	9"	12"
A 4		1¼" x 2	1½" x 2½"	2" x 3½"	2½" x 4½"
A 10	◻	1⅝"	1⅞"	2⅜"	2⅞"
B 2	◻	2⅜"	2⅞"	3⅞"	4⅞"
B 6	◻	1⅝"	1⅞"	2⅜"	2⅞"
B 4		1¼"	1½"	2"	2½"

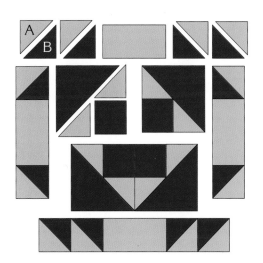

True Blue Quilt Block

HST—pages 12–13

Color/Cut	Subcut	4½"	6"	9"	12"
A 2	▧ ◿	2⅜"	2⅞"	3⅞"	4⅞"
A 1	▢	2"	2½"	3½"	4½"
A 8	▢	1¼"	1½"	2"	2½"
B 2	◼ ◿	2⅜"	2⅞"	3⅞"	4⅞"
B 8	◼	1¼"	1½"	2"	2½"

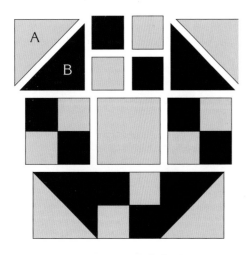

Wagon Tracks

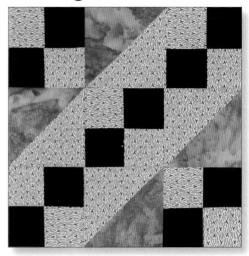

HST—pages 12–13

Color/Cut	Subcut	4½"	6"	9"	12"
A 10	▢		1¼"	1½"	2"	2½"
A 2	▢ ◿	2⅜"	2⅞"	3⅞"	4⅞"
B 2	◼ ◿	2⅜"	2⅞"	3⅞"	4⅞"
C 10	◼	1¼"	1½"	2"	2½"

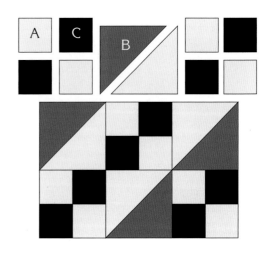

Wampum Block

HST—pages 12–13
Adding Triangles to a Square—page 25

Color/Cut	Subcut	4½"	6"	9"	12"
A 9	◻ ◺	1⅝"	1⅞"	2⅜"	2⅞"
B 3	◼ ◺	1⅝"	1⅞"	2⅜"	2⅞"
C 1	◼	2" x 5"	2½" x 6½"	3½" x 9½"	4½" x 12½"
C 3	◼ ◺	2⅜"	2⅞"	3⅞"	4⅞"

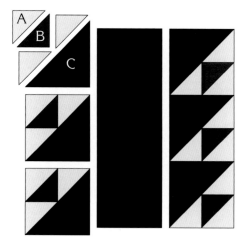

Weathervane Block

HST—pages 12–13
Adding Corners—page 24

Color/Cut	Subcut	4½"	6"	9"	12"
*A 12	▨	1¼"	1½"	2"	2½"
A 4	▨ ◺	1⅝"	1⅞"	2⅜"	2⅞"
B 1	▨	2"	2½"	3½"	4½"
B 4	▨	1¼"	1½"	2"	2½"
B 4	▨ ◺	1⅝"	1⅞"	2⅜"	2⅞"
*C 4	▨	2"	2½"	3½"	4½"

---TIPS---
For Adding Corners on page 24,
use 8-A squares and 4-C squares.

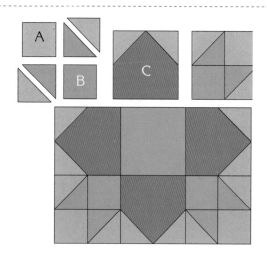

Whirling Pinwheel

HST—pages 12–13

Color/Cut		Subcut	4½"	6"	9"	12"
A 4			1¼"	1½"	2"	2½"
A 12		◻	1⅝"	1⅞"	2⅜"	2⅞"
A 4			1¼" x 2	1½" x 2½"	2" x 3½"	2½" x 4½"
B 12		◻	1⅝"	1⅞"	2⅜"	2⅞"

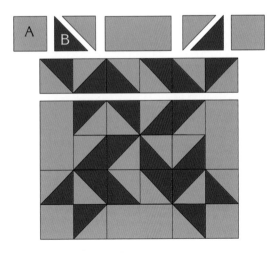

Windblown Block

Color/Cut		Subcut	4½"	6"	9"	12"
A 2			1¼"	1½"	2"	2½"
A 2			1¼" x 2¾"	1½" x 3½"	2" x 5"	2½" x 6½"
A 2			1¼" x 3½"	1½" x 4½"	2" x 6½"	2½" x 8½"
B 4			1¼"	1½"	2"	2½"
C 8			1¼"	1½"	2"	2½"
D 8			1¼"	1½"	2"	2½"

TIPS
Pay attention to your quarter-inch seams to make all these little blocks fit together perfectly.

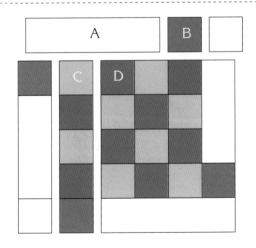

Use this grid to copy and experiment with your own color choices for blocks.

Color Grid

The 7 x 7 Grid Blocks

There are very few traditional blocks in this size, so I decided to design some of my own. Some were inspired by other blocks, like Aunt Sukey's Sister, page 156. If you take a look at Aunt Sukey's Choice, page 137, would you ever think the new block was "related"? I used similar parts but I also increased the block size from a 6 x 6 to 7 x 7 grid block. And sometimes, as I designed, I simply stared at a blank 7 x 7 grid and started coloring.

Ariel Lawn Ball

Designed by Sue Voegtlin

Color/Cut	Subcut	7"	10½"	14"
A 4	☐	2½"	3½"	4½"
A 4	☐	1½"	2"	2½"
A 2	☐	1½" x 2½"	2" x 3½"	2½" x 4½"
A 1	☐	1½" x 4½"	2" x 6½"	2½" x 8½"
A 1	☐	1½" x 5½"	2" x 8"	2½" x 10½"
B 3	▦	1½" x 2½"	2" x 3½"	2½" x 4½"
B 2	▦	1½"	2"	2½
C 4	▪	1½" x 2½"	2" x 3½"	2½" x 4½"

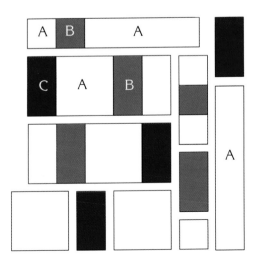

Arrietty's Sugar Cube

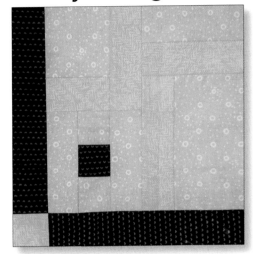

Designed by Sue Voegtlin

Color/Cut	Subcut	7"	10½"	14"
A 1	☐	1½"	2"	2½"
A 1	☐	1½" x 2½"	2 x 3½"	2½" x 4½"
A 2	☐	1½" x 3½"	2 x 5"	2½" x 6½"
A 1	☐	1½" x 4½"	2 x 6½"	2½" x 8½"
B 1	☐	2½"	3½"	4½"
B 2	☐	1½"	2"	2½"
B 3	☐	1½" x 3½"	2 x 5"	2½" x 6½"
B 1	☐	2½" x 4½"	3½" x 6½"	4½" x 8½"
C 2	▪	1½" x 6½"	2 x 9½"	2½" x 12½"
C 1	▪	1½"	2"	2½"

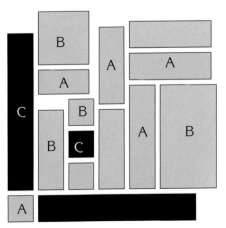

Attention

HST—pages 12-13
Adding Corners—page 24
Designed by Sue Voegtlin

Color/Cut	Subcut		7"	10½"	14"
A 28	☐		1½"	2"	2½"
A 8	☐	◩	1⅞"	2⅜"	2⅞"
B 12	☐		1½"	2"	2½"
B 4	☐		1½" x 2½"	2 x 3½"	2½" x 4½"
C 1	☐		1½"	2"	2½"
D 3	☐		1½" x 2½"	2 x 3½"	2½" x 4½"
D 2	☐	◩	1⅞"	2⅜"	2⅞"

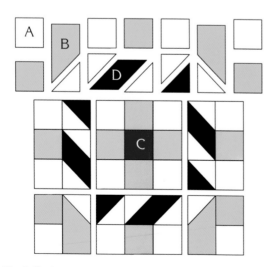

Aunt Sukey's Sister

HST—pages 12-13
Designed by Sue Voegtlin

Color/Cut	Subcut		7"	10½"	14"
A 5	☐		1½"	2"	2½"
A 8	☐	◩	1⅞"	2⅜"	2⅞"
B 2	☐	◩	1⅞"	2⅜"	2⅞"
B 4	☐		1½" x 3½"	2" x 5"	2½" x 6½"
B 4	☐		1½"	2"	2½"
C 8	☐	◩	1⅞"	2⅜"	2⅞"
D 8	☐	◩	1⅞"	2⅜"	2⅞"
D 5	☐		1½"	2"	2½"

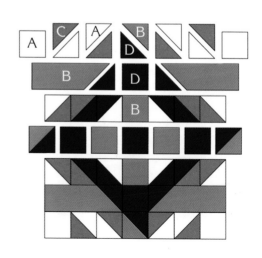

Bear Paws

HST—pages 12-13

Color/Cut	Subcut	7"	10½"	14"
A 8	▢ ◺	1⅞"	2⅜"	2⅞"
A 4	▢	1½"	2"	2½"
A 4	▭	1½" x 3½"	2" x 5"	2½" x 6½"
B 8	▨ ◺	1⅞"	2⅜"	2⅞"
B 8	▨	1½"	2"	2½"
C 4	▨	2½"	3½"	4½"

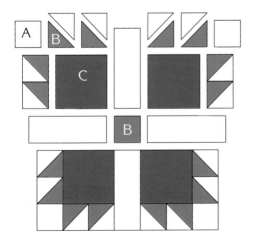

City Center

Designed by Sue Voegtlin

Color/Cut	Subcut	7"	10½"	14"
A 2	▭	1½" x 5½"	2" x 8"	2½" x 10½"
A 2	▭	1½" x 3½"	2" x 5"	2½" x 6½"
A 1	▢	1½"	2"	2½"
B 8	▨	1½"	2"	2½"
C 4	▭	1½" x 3½"	2" x 5"	2½" x 6½"
C 4	▭	1½" x 2½"	2" x 3½"	2½" x 4½"
C 4	▨	1½"	2"	2½"

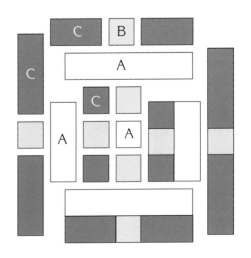

Convergence

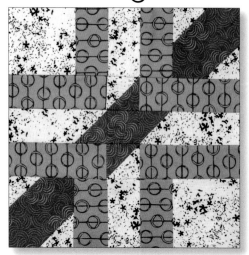

Designed by Sue Voegtlin

Color/Cut	Subcut	7"	10½"	14"
A 2 ☐		2½"	3½"	4½"
A 4 ☐	◺	1⅞"	2⅜"	2⅞"
A 4 ▭		1½" x 2½"	2" x 3½"	2½" x 4½"
B 4 ▭		1½" x 2½"	2" x 3½"	2½" x 4½"
B 4 ▭		1½" x 3½"	2" x 5"	2½" x 6½"
C 4 ■	◺	1⅞"	2⅜"	2⅞"
C 4 ■		1½"	2"	2½"
C 2 ■		2⅞"	3⅞"	4⅞"

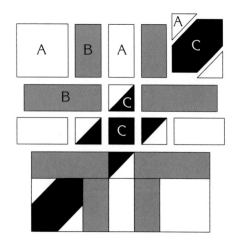

Closed Block

HST—pages 12–13; QST—pages 14–15
Adding Corners—page 24
Designed by Sue Voegtlin

Color/Cut	Subcut	7"	10½"	14"
A 1 ☐	◺	2⅞"	3⅞"	4⅞"
A 2 ☐	⊠	2¼"	2¾"	3¼"
A 4 ☐		2½"	3½"	4½"
A 3 ☐		1½"	2"	2½"
B 1 ■	◺	2⅞"	3⅞"	4⅞"
B 4 ■		1⅞"	2⅜"	2⅞"
B 5 ■		1½"	2"	2½"
B 2 ▬		1½" x 2½"	2" x 3½"	2½" x 4½"
C 2 ■	⊠	2¼"	2¾"	3¼"
C 1 ■	◺	2⅞"	3⅞"	4⅞"
C 2 ■		1½" x 2½"	2" x 3½"	2½" x 4½"

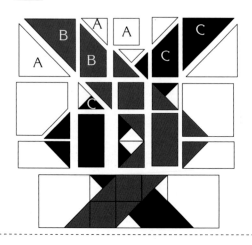

Crazy Eight

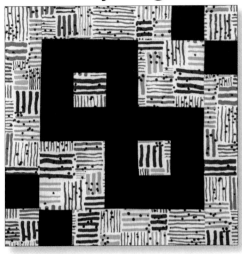

Designed by Sue Voegtlin

Color/Cut	Subcut	7"	10½"	14"
A 2		1½" x 5½"	2" x 8"	2½" x 10½"
A 2		1½" x 4½"	2" x 6½"	2½" x 8½"
A 4		1½"	2"	2½"
A 2		2½"	3½"	4½"
B 8		1½" x 3½"	2" x 5"	2½" x 6½"
B 1		1½" x 3½"	2" x 5"	2½" x 6½

TIPS
It's interesting to see how color can change the look of the Domino block, switching from lights to darks..

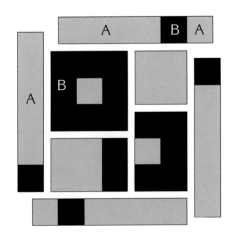

Fenced In

Designed by Sue Voegtlin

Color/Cut	Subcut	7"	10½"	14"
A 10		1⅞"	2⅜"	2⅞"
B 1		1½" x 3½"	2" x 5"	2½" x 6½"
B 10		1⅞"	2⅜"	2⅞"
B 2		1½"	2"	2½"
B 2		2⅞"	3⅞"	4⅞"
C 8		1½"	2"	2½"
C 2		2⅞"	3⅞"	4⅞"

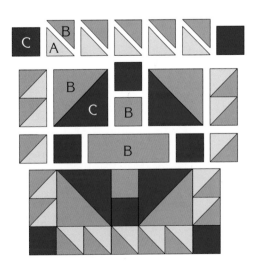

Four of the Same

Designed by Sue Voegtlin

Color/Cut	Subcut	7"	10½"	14"
A 8	▢	1½"	2"	2½"
A 4	▭	1½" x 2½"	2" x 3½"	2½" x 4½"
B 4	▭	1½" x 2½"	2" x 3½"	2½" x 4½"
B 4	▭	1½" x 3½"	2" x 5"	2½" x 6½"
C 8	▢	1½"	2"	2½"
C 1	▭	1½" x 5½"	2" x 8"	2½" x 10½"

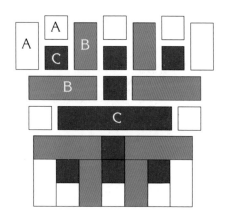

Good N' Plenty

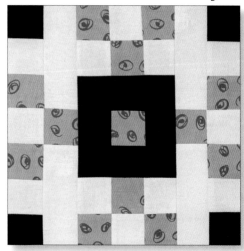

Designed by Sue Voegtlin

Color/Cut	Subcut	7"	10½"	14"
A 12	▢	1½"	2"	2½"
A 4	▭	1½" x 3½"	2" x 5"	2½" x 6½"
B 13	▢	1½"	2"	2½"
C 6	▢	1½"	2"	2½"
C 2	▭	1½" x 3½"	2" x 5"	2½" x 6½"

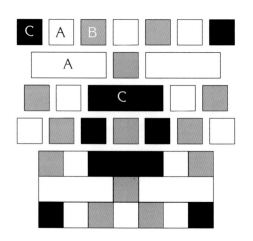

Hens and Chicks

HST—pages 12-13

Color/Cut	Subcut	7"	10½"	14"
A 10	◰ ◿	1⅞"	2⅜"	2⅞"
B 4	▢	2½"	3½"	4½"
C 2	▭	1½" x 3½"	2 "x 5"	2½" x 6½"
C 1	▭	1½" x 7½"	2" x 11"	2½" x 14½"
D 10	◼ ◿	1⅞"	2⅜"	2⅞"

---TIPS---
Pay attention orientation of HSTs.

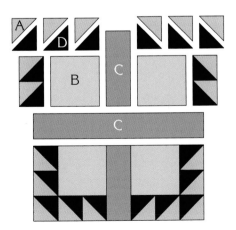

Layered Squares

HST—pages 12-13
Designed by Sue Voegtlin

Color/Cut	Subcut	7"	10½"	14"
A 2	▭	1½" x 2½"	2" x 3½"	2½" x 4½"
A 3	▭	1½" x 3½"	2" x 5"	2½" x 6½"
A 2	▭	1½" x 4½"	2" x 6½"	2½" x 8½"
A 2	▢	1½"	2"	2½"
A 1	▢	2½"	3½"	4½"
B 2	◼	1½"	2"	2½"
B 4	◼	1½" x 3½"	2" x 5	2½" x 6½"
C 1	◼	1½"	2"	2½"
C 4	◼	1½" x 2½"	2" x 3½"	2½" x 4½
C 1	◼	1½" x 3½"	2" x 5"	2½" x 6½"

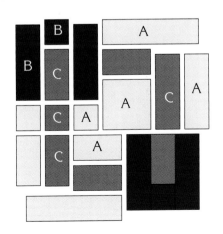

Lincoln's Platform

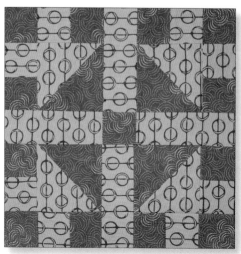

HST—pages 12–13
Designed by Sue Voegtlin

Color/Cut	Subcut	7"	10½"	14"
A 2		2⅞"	3⅞"	4⅞"
A 10		1½"	2"	2½"
A 4		1½" x 3½"	2" x 5"	2½" x 6½"
B 2		2⅞"	3⅞"	4⅞"
B 13		1½"	2"	2½"

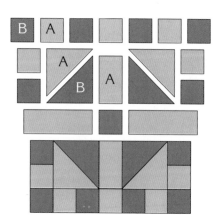

Linked Rectangles

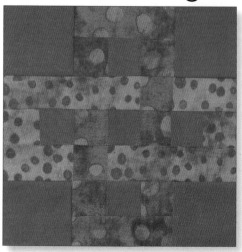

Designed by Sue Voegtlin

Color/Cut	Subcut	7"	10½"	14"
A 2		1½"	2"	2½"
A 2		1½" x2½"	2" x3½"	2½" x 4½"
A 2		1½" x 4½"	2 x 6½"	2½" x 8½"
B 5		1½"	2"	2½"
B 4		2½"	3½"	4½"
C 8		1½"	2"	2½"
C 2		1½" x 3½"	2" x 5"	2½" x 6½"

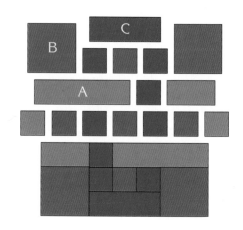

Linked Squares

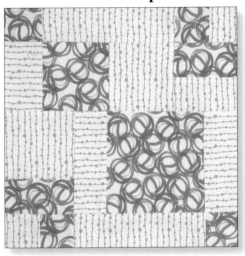

Designed by Sue Voegtlin

Color/Cut	Subcut	7"	10½"	14"
A 2		1½" x 4½"	2 x 6½"	2½" x 8½"
A 2		1½" x 2½"	2 x 3½"	2½" x 4½"
A 2		1½"	2"	2½"
A 2		2½"	3½"	4½"
A 2		1½" x 3½"	2" x 5"	2½" x 6½"
B 1		2½"	3½"	4½"
B 2		1½" x 2½"	2 x 3½"	2½" x 4½"
B 4		1½"	2"	2½"
B 1		3½"	5	6½"

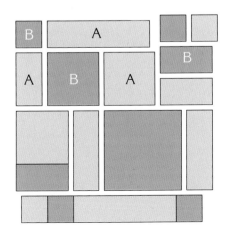

Middleground

Designed by Sue Voegtlin

Color/Cut	Subcut	7"	10½"	14"
A 2		1½" x 3½"	2" x 5	2½" x 6½"
A 2		1½"	2"	2½"
B 8		1½"	2"	2½"
C 2		1½" x 3½"	2" x 5	2½" x 6½"
C 2		1½" x 5½"	2 x 8	2½" x10½"
C 4		1½"	2"	2½"
D 8		1½" x 2½"	2" x 3½"	2½" x 4½"
E 1		1½"	2"	2½"

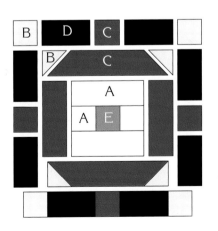

Open

Adding Corners—page 24
Designed by Sue Voegtlin

Color/Cut	Subcut	7"	10½"	14"
A 3		2½"	3½"	4½"
A 4		1½" x 2½"	2" x 3½"	2½" x 4½"
A 12		1½"	2"	2½"
A 1		1½" x 3½"	2 x 5	2½" x 6½"
B 5		1½"	2"	2½"
B 3		2½"	3½"	4½"
C 1		1½" x 2½"	2" x 3½"	2½" x 4½"
C 7		1½"	2"	2½"
C 3		2½"	3½"	4½"

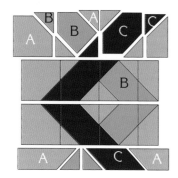

Point Taken

HST—pages 12–13
Designed by Sue Voegtlin

Color/Cut	Subcut	7"	10½"	14"
A 1		2½"	3½"	4½"
A 3	◻	2⅞"	3⅞"	4⅞"
A 6		1½"	2"	2½"
A 2		1½" x 2½"	2" x 3½"	2½" x 4½"
A 1		1½" x 5½"	2" x 8"	2½" x 10½"
B 3		1½"	2"	2½"
B 3	◻	2⅞"	3⅞"	4⅞"

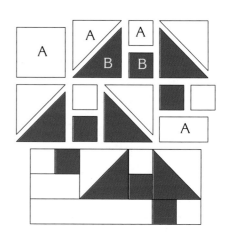

Quaking Columns

HST—pages 12–13
Adding Corners—page 24
Designed by Sue Voegtlin

Color/Cut	Subcut	7"	10½"	14"
A 4		1⅞"	2⅜"	2⅞"
A 4		2½" x 3½"	3½" x 5	4½" x 6½"
B 1		2¼"	2¾"	3¼"
B 8		1½"	2	2½"
B 6		1⅞"	2⅜"	2⅞"
C 13		1½"	2	2½"
C 1		2¼"	2¾"	3¼"

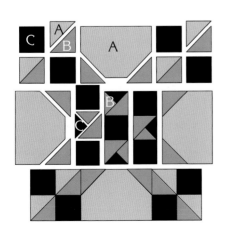

Scattered Block

Designed by Sue Voegtlin

Color/Cut	Subcut	7"	10½"	14"
A 7		1½" x 2½"	2 x 3½"	2½" x 4½"
A 1		1½" x 3½"	2 x 5	2½" x 6½"
A 1		2½"	3½"	4½"
A 4		2⅞"	3⅞"	4⅞"

4-5 Assorted colors for:

Color/Cut	Subcut	7"	10½"	14"
B 4		2⅞"	3⅞"	4⅞"

Mix or match HSTs for the block and use any extras for another project.

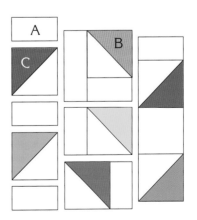

The 7 x 7 Grid Blocks

Tattersall Block

Designed by Sue Voegtlin

Color/Cut	Subcut	7"	10½"	14"
A 8		1½"	2	2½"
B 8		1½"	2	2½"
C 6		1½" x 2½"	2" x 3½"	2½" x 4½"
C 2		1½" x 7½"	2 x 11	2½" x 14½"

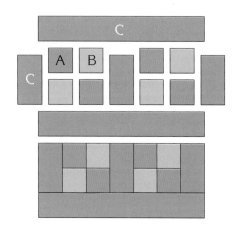

Three Crosses

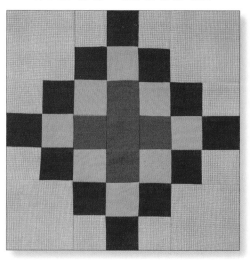

Color/Cut	Subcut	7"	10½"	14"
A 8		1½"	2"	2½"
B 12		1½"	2"	2½"
C 2		1½"	2"	2½"
C 1		1½" x 3½"	2" x 5"	2½" x 6½"
D 4		2½"	3½"	4½"
D 8		1½"	2"	2½"

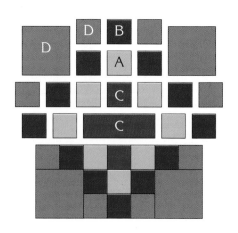

Tuning Fork

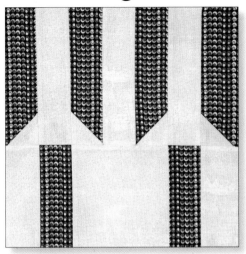

Adding Corners—page 24
Designed by Sue Voegtlin

Color/Cut	Subcut	7"	10½"	14"
A 3		1½" x 4½"	2" x 6½"	2½" x 8½"
A 2		1½" x 3½"	2" x 5"	2½" x 6½"
A 1		3½"	5	6½"
B 2		1½" x 3½"	2" x 5"	2½" x 6½"
B 4		1½" x 4½"	2" x 6½"	2½" x 8½"

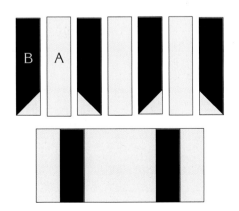

Twisted Ribbon

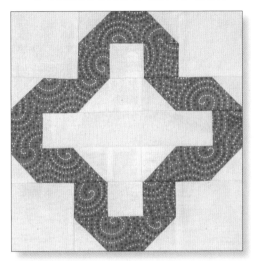

Parallel Seams—page 22

Color/Cut	Subcut	7"	10½"	14"
A 4		2½"	3½"	4½"
A 16		1½"	2"	2½"
A 1		1½" x5½"	2 x 8"	2½" x 10½"
B 6		1½"	2"	2½"
B 6		1½" x 3½"	2" x 5"	2½" x 6½"

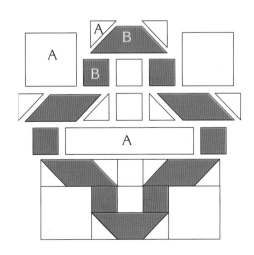

The 7 x 7 Grid Blocks

Windblown Tree

Adding Corners—page 24
Designed by Sue Voegtlin

Color/Cut	Subcut	7"	10½"	14"
A 15		1½"	2½"	3½"
A 2		1½" x 3½"	2½" x 6½"	3½" x 9½"
A 5		1½" x 2½"	2" x 3½"	2½" x 4½"
B 1		1½"	2½"	3½"

From assorted batik or colors of your choice, cut:

1		1½" x 3½"	2" x 5"	2½" x 6½"
2		1½" x 5½"	2" x 8"	2½" x 10½"
1		1½" x 4½"	2" x 6½"	2½" x 8½"
2		1½" x 6½"	2" x 9½"	2½" x 12½"

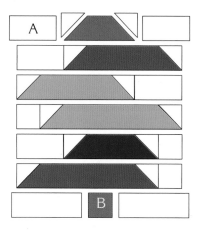

Winning Lucky 7

*For Adding Corners on page 24, use squares and rectangles.
Designed by Sue Voegtlin

Color/Cut	Subcut	7"	10½"	14"
A 1		2⅞"	3⅞"	4⅞"
A 2		1½" x 2½"	2 x 3½"	2½" x 4½"
A 11		1½"	2½"	3½"
A 1		2½"	3½"	4½"
B 1		2⅞"	3⅞"	4⅞"
B 1		1½" x 3½"	2 x 5	2½" x 6½"
B 3		1½"	2½"	3½"
C 1		2⅞"	3⅞"	4⅞"
C 2		1½" x 2½"	2 x 3½"	2½" x 4½"
C 2		2½"	3½"	4½"
C 3		1½"	2½"	3½"
D 1		2½"	3½"	4½"
D 1		2⅞"	3⅞"	4⅞"
D 3		1½"	2"	2½"

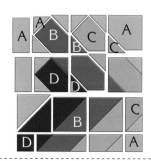

The 8 x 8 Grid Blocks

Dimensionally, this grid size is part a of two, four, and six grid base category. I designed Chinook Wind, page 171, and you can see if you take away the borders it becomes a block on its own, based on the 6 x 6 grid. By studying blocks, you will start to see how some simple changes can create new blocks of your own design.

Century in Progress

Color/Cut	Subcut		8"	12"	16"
A 1	▪		1½"	2"	2½"
A 1	▪		1½" x 3½"	2" x 5"	2½" x 6½"
A 1	▪		2½" x 5½"	3½" x 8½"	4½" x 10½"
B 1	▪		1½" x 7½"	2" x 11"	2½" x 14½"
B 1	▪		2½" x 3½"	3½" x 5"	4½" x 6½"
C 1	▪		2½" x 3½"	3½" x 5"	4½" x 6½"
D 1	▪		2½"	3½"	4½"
E 1	▪		4½" x 5½"	6½" x 8½"	8½" x 10½"
F 1	▪		1½" x7½"	2" x11"	2½" x 14½"

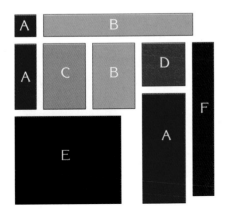

Chinook Wind

HST—pages 12-13

Color/Cut	Subcut		8"	12"	16"
A 12	▪		1½"	2"	2½"
A 2	▪	◹	2⅞"	3⅞"	4⅞"
B 2	▪	◹	2⅞"	3⅞"	4⅞"
B 8	▪		1½"	2"	2½"
C 4	▪		1½" x 6½"	2" x 9½"	2½" x 12½"
D 1	▪		2½"	3½"	4½"

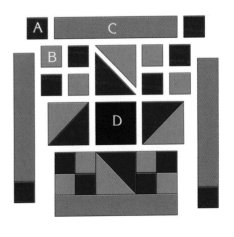

Cog Wheels

Color/Cut	Subcut	8"	12"	16"
A 16		1½"	2"	2½"
A 4		2½"	3½"	4½"
B 16		1½"	2"	2½"
B 4		2½"	3½"	4½"

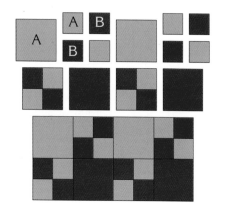

Cross and Diamonds

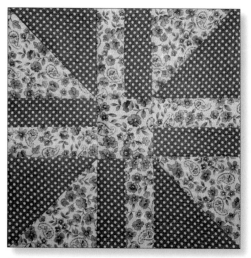

HST—pages 12–13

Color/Cut	Subcut	8"	12"	16"
A 2	◿	3⅞"	5⅜"	6⅞"
A 1		2½"	3½"	4½"
A 4		1½" x 3½"	2" x 5"	2½" x 6½"
B 2	◹	3⅞"	5⅜"	6⅞"
B 4		1½" x 3½"	2" x 5"	2½" x 6½"

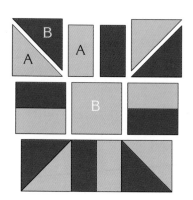

Dan's Mountain

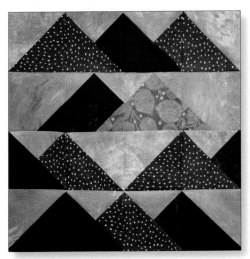

HST—pages 12–13
3-Patch HST—page 27
Designed by Sue Voegtlin

Color/Cut	Subcut	8"	12"	16"
A 3		2⅞"	3⅞"	4⅞"
A 2		3¼"	4¼"	5¼"
A 2		2½"	3½"	4½"
A 2		1⅞"	2⅜"	2⅞"
B 4		2⅞"	3⅞"	4⅞"
B 1		3¼"	4¼"	5¼"
C 3		2⅞"	3⅞"	4⅞"
C 1		3¼"	4¼"	5¼"
C 1		1½"	2"	2½"
C 1		2½"	3½"	4½"
D 1		2½"	3½"	4½"
D 2		1½"	2"	2½"

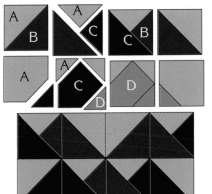

Every Town Square

Adding Corners—page 24
Adding Triangles to a Square—page 25
Designed by Sue Voegtlin

Color/Cut	Subcut	8"	12"	16"
A 12		1½"	2½"	3½"
B 4		1⅞"	2⅜"	3⅞"
B 8		1½" x 2½"	2" x 3½"	2½" x 4½"
C 4		1⅞"	2⅜"	2⅞"
C 4		2½"	3½"	4½"
C 4		1½" x 2½"	2" x 3½"	2½" x 4½"
D 4		1½" x 2½"	2" x 3½"	2½" x 4½"

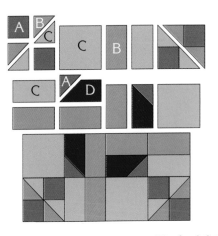

Fair Sign

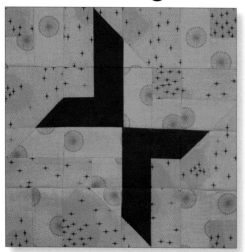

Adding Corners—page 24
Designed by Sue Voegtlin

Color/Cut	Subcut	8"	12"	16"
A 12		1½"	2"	2½"
A 4		2½"	3½"	4½"
A 6		1½" x 2½"	2" x 3½"	2½" x 4½"
B 8		1½"	2"	3½"
B 8		1½" x 2½"	2" x 3½"	2½" x 4½"
C 4		1½"	2"	2½"
C 4		1½" x 2½"	2" x 3½"	2½" x 4½"

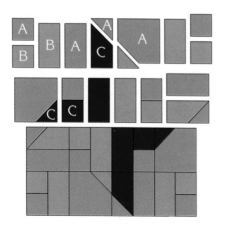

First Nation Chief

Adding Corners—page 24

Color/Cut	Subcut	8"	12"	16"
A 4		2½" x4½"	3½" x 6½"	4½" x 8½"
A 12		1½"	2"	2½"
B 2		1½" x 3½"	2" x 5"	2½" x 6½"
B 2		1½" x 4½"	2" x 6½"	2½" x 8½"
C 2		1½" x 3½"	2" x 5"	2½" x 6½"
B 2		1½" x 4½"	2" x 6½"	2½" x 8½"
D 4		1½"	2"	2½"

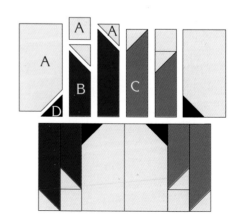

Formosa

Color/Cut	Subcut	8"	12"	16"
A 4	⬜	2½"	3½"	4½"
B 4	⬛	1½" x 2½"	2" x 3½"	2½" x 4½"
B 4	⬛	2½"	3½"	4½"
C 4	⬛	1½" x 2½"	2" x 3½"	2½" x4½"
C 4	⬛	1½" x 3½"	2" x 5"	2½" x 6½"
C 1	⬛	2½"	3½"	4½"

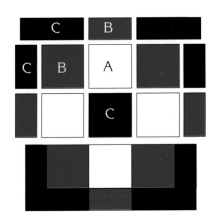

Four Way Stop

Adding Corners—page 24
Designed by Sue Voegtlin

Color/Cut	Subcut	8"	12"	16"
A 4	⬜ ⬜	3½"	5"	6½"
B 8	▨	1½"	2"	2½"
B 4	▨	1½" x 3½"	2" x 5"	2½" x 6½"
B 4	▨	2½"	3½"	4½"
C 1	⬛	2½"	3½"	4½"
C 4	⬛	1½" x 2½"	2" x 3½"	2½" x 4½"

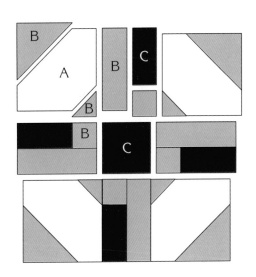

Garden Path

Adding Corners—page 24

Color/Cut	Subcut	8"	12"	16"
A 8		2½"	3½"	4½"
A 2	◻	2¼"	3"	3⅝"
B 24		1½"	2"	2½"
C 2	◻	2⅞"	3⅞"	4⅞"
D 5		2½"	3½"	4½"

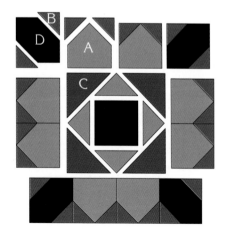

Glitter Top

Color/Cut	Subcut	8"	12"	16"
A 16		1½"	2"	2½"
*A 8		1⅞"	2⅜"	2⅞"
A 4		2½"	3½"	4½"
*B 2		3¼"	4¼"	5¼"
B 4		1½" x 2½"	2" x 3½"	2½" x 4½"
B 5		2½"	3½"	4½"
B 4		½"	2"	2½"

----- TIPS -----
*Use 8-A and 2-B squares to make Four-at-a-Time Flying Geese—page 18.

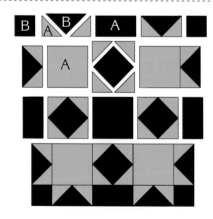

In a Roundabout Way

HST—pages 12-13
Designed by Sue Voegtlin

Color/Cut	Subcut	8"	12"	16"
A 6	☐	1½"	2"	2½"
A 2	☐◹	1⅞"	2⅜"	2⅞"
A 4	▭	1½" x 2½"	2" x 3½"	2½" x 4½"
A 2	▭	1½" x 5-½"	2" x 8"	2½" x 10½"
B 1	◼	2½"	3½"	4½"
B 4	▬	1½" x 2½"	2" x 3½"	2½" x 4½"
C 4	◼	1½"	2"	2½"
C 2	◼◹	1⅞"	2⅜"	2⅞"
C 2	◼◹	2⅞"	3⅞"	4⅞"
C 2	▬	1½" x 2½"	2" x 3½"	2½" x 4½"

In the Center

HST—pages 12-13
Designed by Sue Voegtlin

Color/Cut	Subcut	8"	12"	16"
A 1	☐	4½"	6½"	8½"
A 12	▭	1½" x 2½"	2" x 3½"	2½" x 4½"
A 8	☐	1½"	2"	2½"
B 8	◼	1½"	2"	2½"
B 4	▬	1½" x 2½"	2" x 3½"	2½" x 4½"
C 8	◼	1½"	2"	2½"
C 4	▬	1½" x 2½"	2" x 3½"	2½" x 4½"

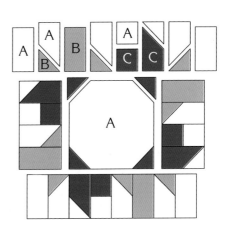

Jester's Patch

*QST Technique 1, page 14, steps 1–2.
Designed by Sue Voegtlin

Color/Cut	Subcut	8"	12"	16"
*A 1 	⊠	5¼"	7¼"	9¼"
*B 1		5¼"	7¼"	9¼"
B 2		3⅜"	4¾"	6⅛"
*C 1	⊠	5¼"	7¼"	9¼"
C 2		3⅜"	4¾"	6⅛"

TIPS
*You will have extra pieces.

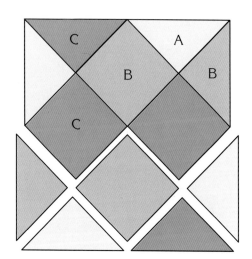

Kitchen Aid

Partial Seams—page 20
Adding Corners—page 24
Designed by Sue Voegtlin

Color/Cut	Subcut	8"	12"	16"
A 4		2½" x 6½"	3½" x 9½"	4½" x 12½"
B 8		2½"	3½"	4½"
C 4		2½"	3½"	4½"
D 1		4½"	6½"	8½"

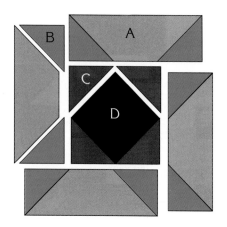

Lightning Block

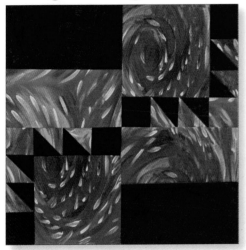

HST—pages 12-13

Color/Cut	Subcut	8"	12"	16"
A 4	◻	1⅞"	2⅜"	2⅞"
A 2		2½" x 4½"	3½" x 6½"	4½" x 8½"
A 2		1½"	2"	2½"
A 2		3½"	5"	6½"
B 4	◻	1⅞"	2⅜"	2⅞"
B 2		2½" x 4½"	3½" x 6½"	4½" x 8½"
B 4		1½"	2"	2½"

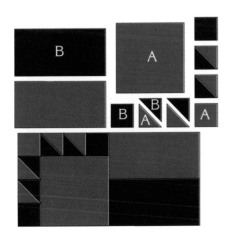

Log Cabin

Color/Cut	Subcut	8"	12"	16"
A 2		1½" x 2½"	2" x 3½"	2½" x 4½"
A 2		1½" x 4½"	2" x 6½"	2½" x 8½"
A 2		1½" x 6½"	2" x 9½"	2½" x 12½"
B 1		2½"	3½"	4½"
C 2		1½" x 8½"	2" x 12½"	2½" x 16½"
C 2		1½" x 6½"	2" x 9½"	2½" x 12½"
C 2		1½" x 4½"	2" x 6½"	2½" x 8½"

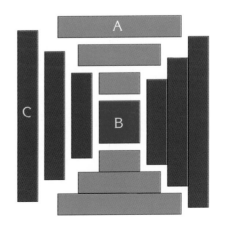

Mosaic 7

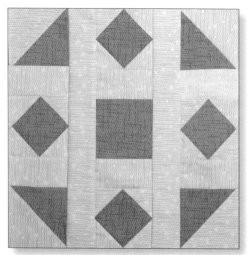

Adding Corners—page 24

Color/Cut	Subcut	8"	12"	16"
A 16		1½"	2"	2½"
A 2	◺	2⅞"	3⅞"	4⅞"
A 2		1½" x 8½"	2" x 12½"	2½" x 16½"
A 6		1½" x 2½"	2" x 3½"	2½" x 4½"
B 2	◹	2⅞"	3⅞"	4⅞"
B 5		2½"	3½"	4½"

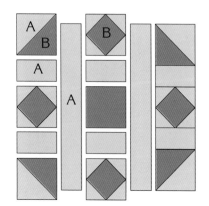

Orion's Stars

HST—pages 12–13
Designed by Sue Voegtlin

Color/Cut	Subcut	8"	12"	16"
A 4		1½"	2"	2½"
A 12	◺	1⅞"	2⅜"	2⅞"
A 4		1½" x 3½"	2" x 5"	2½" x 6½"
B 4	◺	1⅞"	2⅜"	2⅞"
C 4	◺	1⅞"	2⅜"	2⅞"
D 4	◺	1⅞"	2⅜"	2⅞"
E 4	◺	1⅞"	2⅜"	2⅞"
F 4		2½"	3½"	4½"
F 4		1½"	2"	2½"

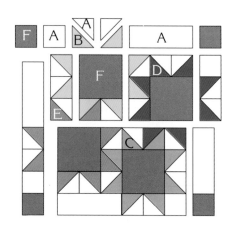

Redwood Block

HST—pages 12–13

Color/Cut	Subcut	8"	12"	16"
A 10		1½"	2"	2½"
A 2		2½"	3½"	4½"
A 4		1½" x 2½"	2" x 3½"	2½" x 4½
B 1		2½"	3½"	4½"
B 2		1½"	2"	2½"
C 3		1½"	2"	2½"
C 4		1½" x 2½"	2" x 3½"	2½" x 4½"
D 2		1½" x 2½"	2" x 3½"	2½" x4½"
D 5		1½"	2"	2½"
E 4		1½"	2"	2½"
E 2		1½" x 2½"	2" x 3½"	2½" x4½"
F 2		2½"	3½"	4½"
F 5		1½"	2"	2½"

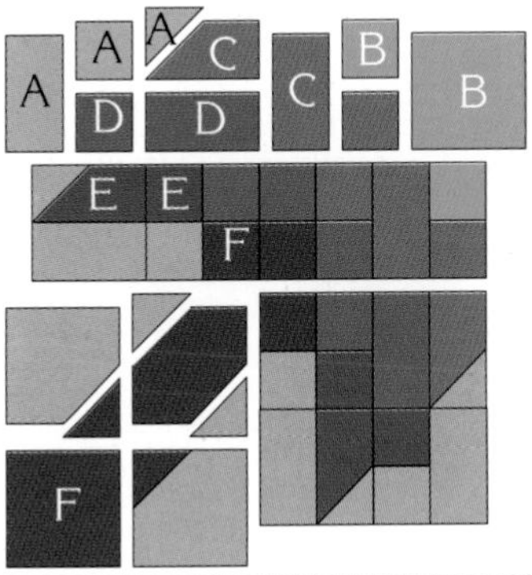

Rising Sun

QST—page 14
HST—page 12–13
Adding Corners—page 24

Color/Cut	Subcut	8"	12"	16"
A 2		1⅞"	2⅜"	2⅞"
A 2		3¼"	4¼"	5¼"
A 4		2½"	3½"	4½"
A 8		1½" x 2½"	2" x 3½"	2½" x 4½"
B 8		1½"	2"	2½"
B 2		3¼"	4¼"	5¼"
B 2		1⅞"	2⅜"	2⅞"
B 1		2½"	3½"	4½"
C 4		1½" x 2½"	2" x 3½"	2½" x 4½"

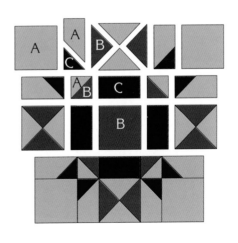

The 8 x 8 Grid Blocks

Round a What

Adding Corners—page 24
Designed by Sue Voegtlin

Color/Cut	Subcut	8"	12"	16"
A 4		2½"	3½"	4½"
A 4		1½" x 3½"	2" x 5"	2½" x 6½"
B 4		1½" x 3½"	2" x 5"	2½" x 6½"
B 4		2½" x4½"	3½" x 6½"	4½" x 8½"
C 8		1½"	2"	2½"

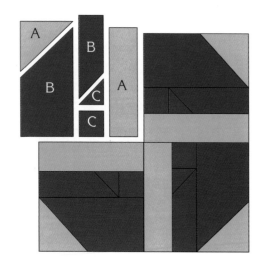

Slightly Off Center

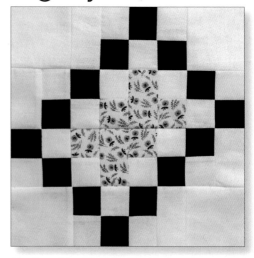

Designed by Sue Voegtlin

Color/Cut	Subcut	8"	12"	16"
A 4		2½"	3½"	4½"
A 18		1½"	2"	2½"
A 4		1½" x 2½"	2" x 3½"	2½" x 4½"
B 4		1½"	2"	2½"
B 2		1½" x 2½"	2" x 3½"	2½" x 4½"
C 14		1½"	2"	2½"

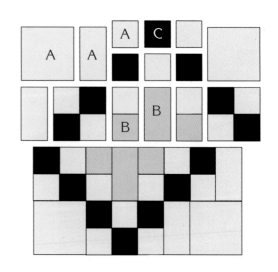

Starry Path

QST Technique 1—page 14, steps 1–2

Color/Cut		Subcut	8"	12"	16"
A 1		⊠	7¼"	10¼"	13¼"
A 4		⊠	2⅞"	3⅞"	4⅞"
B 1		⊠	7¼"	10¼"	13¼"
B 4		⊠	2⅞"	3⅞"	4⅞"

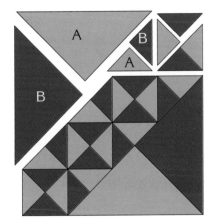

Summer Breezes

Parallel Seams—page 14

Color/Cut		Subcut	8"	12"	16"
A 4			2½"	3½"	4½"
B 8			1½"	2"	2½"
B 5			2½"	3½"	4½"
C 4			2½"	3½"	4½"
C 4			1½" x 3½"	2" x 5"	2½" x 6½"

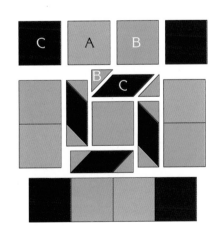

T Quilt

Adding Corners—page 24

Color/Cut	Subcut	8"	12"	16"
A 8		1½" x 3½"	2" x 5½"	2½" x 6½"
A 8		1½"	2"	2½"
B 8		2" x 3½"	2½" x 5"	3" x 6½"

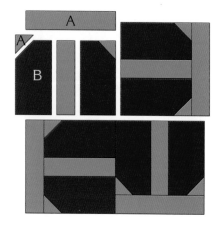

The Exquisite

Adding Corners—page 24

Color/Cut	Subcut	8"	12"	16"
A 16		2½"	3½"	4½"
B 32		1½"	2"	2½"

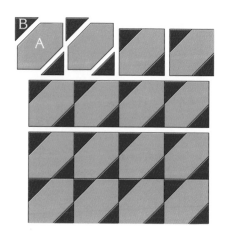

The Swallow

HST—pages 12–13
Adding Corners—page 24

Color/Cut	Subcut	8"	12"	16"
A 2	◩	2⅞"	3⅞"	4⅞"
A 2		2½" x 4½"	3½" x 6½"	4½" x 8½"
A 1		3½"	5"	6½"
A 1	◩	4⅞"	6⅞"	8⅞"
B 1	◩	1⅞"	2⅜"	2⅞"
B 2		1½" x 4½"	2" x 6½"	2½" x 8½"
B 2		1½" x 3½"	2" x 5"	2½" x 6½"
B 4		2½"	3½"	4½"
B 3	◩	2⅞"	3⅞"	4⅞"

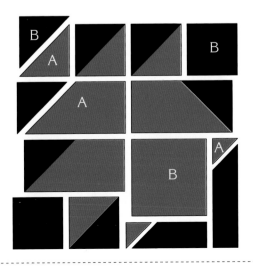

Thistle

Designed by Sue Voegtlin

Color/Cut	Subcut	8"	12"	16"
A 4		2½"	3½"	4½"
A 5	◩	2⅞"	3⅞"	4⅞"
A 2	◩	1⅞"	2⅜"	3⅞"
B 5	◩	2⅞"	3⅞"	4⅞"
B 2		2½"	3½"	4½"
B 4		1½"	2"	2½"

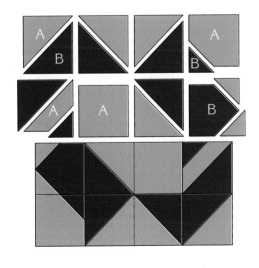

The 8 x 8 Grid Blocks

Trashed Hash

Designed by Sue Voegtlin

Color/Cut	Subcut	8"	12"	16"
A 2		1½" x 4½"	2" x 6½"	2½" x 8½"
A 2		1½" x 2½"	2" x 3½"	2½" x 4½"
B 2		1½" x 4½"	2" x 6½"	2½" x 8½"
B 2		1½" x 2½"	2" x 3½"	2½" x 4½"
C 9		2½"	3½"	4½"
C 4		1½"	2"	2½"

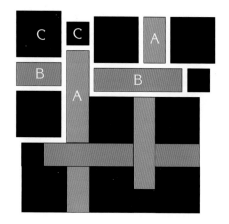

True Lover's Knot

Adding Corners—page 24

Color/Cut	Subcut	8"	12"	16"
A 4		2½"	3½"	4½"
A 1		4½"	6½"	8½"
B 4		2½" x 4½"	3½" x 6½"	4½" x 8½"
C 16		1½"	2"	2½"

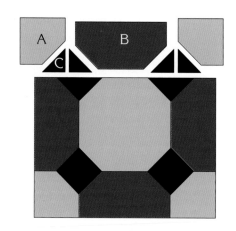

Tulip Lady Finger

HST—pages 12–13

Color/Cut	Subcut	8"	12"	16"
A 4		1½"	2"	3½"
A 4	◻◺	1⅞"	2⅜"	2⅞"
A 4		2½" x 4½"	3½" x 6½"	4½" x 8½"
B 4	◻◺	1⅞"	2⅜"	2⅞"
B 4		1½"	2"	3½"
B 1		4½"	6½"	8½"

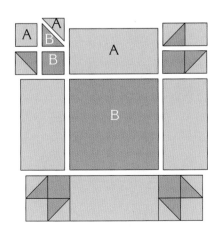

Twin Darts

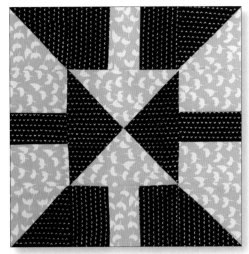

HST—pages 12–13
QST Technique 1—page 14, steps 1–3

Color/Cut	Subcut	8"	12"	16"
A 2	◻⧄	2⅞"	3⅞"	4⅞"
A 1	◻⧅	4⅞"	6⅞"	8⅞"
A 2		1½" x 2½"	2½ x 3½"	2½" x 4½"
A 4		2" x 2½"	2½ x 3½"	3½" x 4½"
B 2	◻⧄	2⅞"	3⅞"	4⅞"
B 1	◻⧅	4⅞"	6⅞"	8⅞"
B 2		1½" x 2½"	2½ x 3½"	2½" x 4½"
B 4		2" x 2½"	2½ x 3½"	3½" x 4½"

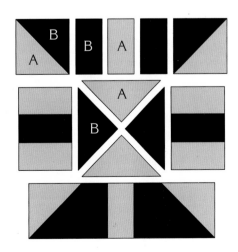

Which Way

Designed by Sue Voegtlin

Color/Cut	Subcut	8"	12"	16"
A 6	▭	1½" x 2½"	2" x 3½"	2½" x 4½"
A 3	▭	1½" x 3½"	2" x 5	2½" x 6½"
A 1	▭	1½" x 4½"	2" x 6½"	2½" x 8½
B 8	■	1½"	2"	2½"
C 1	▬	1½" x 2½"	2" x 3½"	2½" x 4½"
C 3	▬	1½" x 3½"	2" x 5"	2½" x 6½"
C 1	▬	1½" x 4½"	2" x 6½"	2½" x 8½"
C 1	■	1½"	2"	2½"
D 2	■	1½"	2"	2½"
D 3	▬	1½" x 3½"	2" x 5"	2½" x 6½"
D 1	▬	1½" x 4½"	2" x 6½"	2½" x 8½"

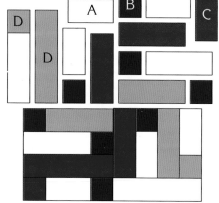

Whirling Dervish

HST—pages 12–13
Adding Corners—page 24
Designed by Sue Voegtlin

Color/Cut	Subcut	8"	12"	16"
A 4	▭	1½" x 2½"	2" x 3½"	2½" x 4½"
A 4	☐	2½"	3½"	4½"
A 12	☐	1½"	2"	2½"
A 4	☐	2⅞"	3⅞"	4⅞"
B 8	■	1½"	2"	2½"
B 4	◩	2⅞"	3⅞"	4⅞"
C 4	■	1½"	2"	2½"

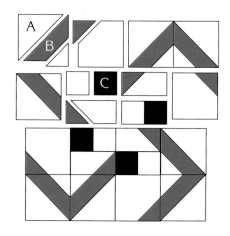

Use this grid to copy and experiment with your own color choices for blocks.

Color Grid

Settings and Charts

Have you made blocks and want to arrange them in a quilt setting? Here are four options to consider. You may choose to make an entire quilt but these settings could also be used for smaller projects like a lap quilt, table runner, or even a wallhanging. I included coloring pages for you to copy and experiment with your own color choices.

If you have made favorite blocks that you want to showcase in a single project, try a quilt sampler. If you made blocks from different grid sizes, it might be a good idea to separate them with sashing. Grid sizes divisible by 2 work well together because the seams and pieces will match up evenly. A 3-grid block sitting next to a 4-grid block doesn't work as well because of the difference in seam alignment. Sashing will not only set each block apart but it will downplay the differences.

STRAIGHT SETTING

The setting below includes sashing with cornerstones, however, a straight setting can also be:

- Block-to-Block

- Alternate (block and setting squares)

- Alternate block (two block designs, arranged every other one)

- Sashing (continuous sashing, sashing with cornerstones, pieced sashing)

Flock of Geese
2 x 2
Page 33

Straight Setting

ON-POINT SETTING

An on-point, or diagonal setting simply means the blocks are set at a 45° angle, with side and corner setting triangles. The setting shown here is set block-to-block, creating an interesting secondary pattern where the corner squares create a four-patch. Blocks can also be set on-point using alternate blocks or with sashing.

Aunt Sukey's Choice is a block that changes drastically depending on color placement, where you place the darkest and lightest values, and how you set the blocks. Make a copy of the line drawing on page 137 and play around with value and color placement. You might design a completely new quilt!

Aunt Sukey's Choice
6 x 6
Page 137

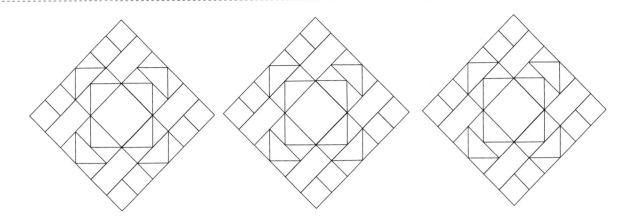

MEDALLION SETTING

A traditional medallion setting has a center focal block or design, often set on-point, with multiple (pieced and non-pieced) borders or frames added around it. The pieced borders of a medallion quilt often incorporate quilt blocks.

The setting I created is a modern, or contemporary medallion, pieced using more of the same block but varying the sashing and borders to highlight the center medallion. Notice how the Homeward Bound block is one of those blocks that can create secondary patterns and even new block designs.

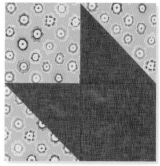

Homeward Bound
2 x 2
Page 36

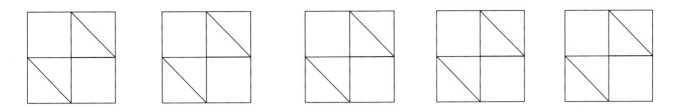

ASYMMETRICAL SETTING

Non-traditional settings have been used by makers of utility quilts for decades (i.e. Gee's Bend quilters, frontier women and housewives re-purposing clothing scraps.) More recently, modern quilters have embraced the non-traditional, asymmetrical layouts with more negative space and simple design elements. These non-traditional settings may or may not incorporate quilt "blocks." The setting below is one example of how a traditional block, Patience Corners, can be colored and set in a very modern way.

Patience Corners
4 x 4
Page 97

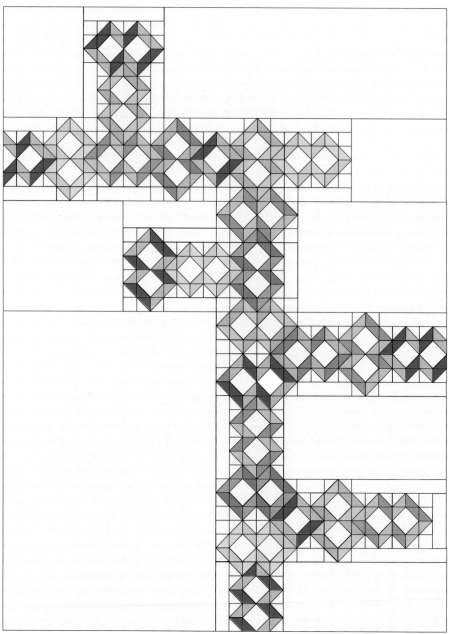

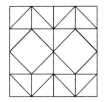 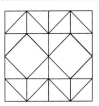 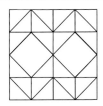 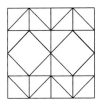 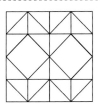

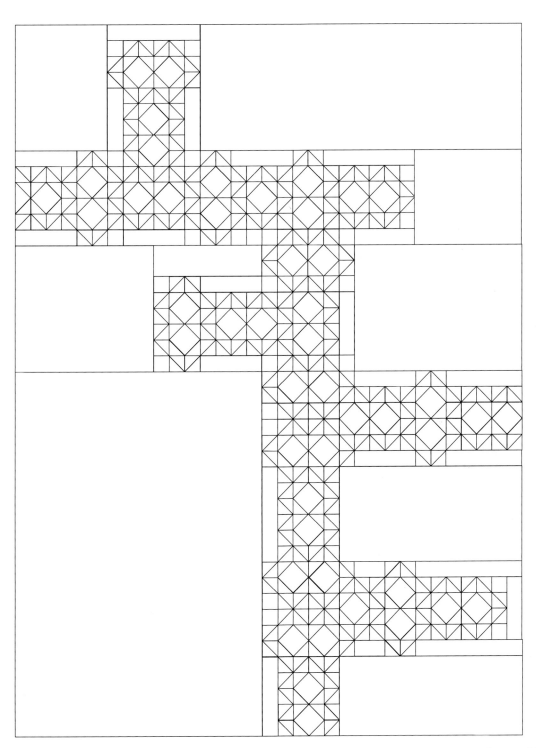

Asymmetrical Setting

SAMPLER SETTING

The illustration below shows how I used some of my blocks to make a quilt sampler. I used grid paper and sketched out block placement in a square quilt size. Start with any quilt shape or size and use your own block. They can all be the same size or you can mix the sizes, too. This is your opportunity to create a quilt design of your own.

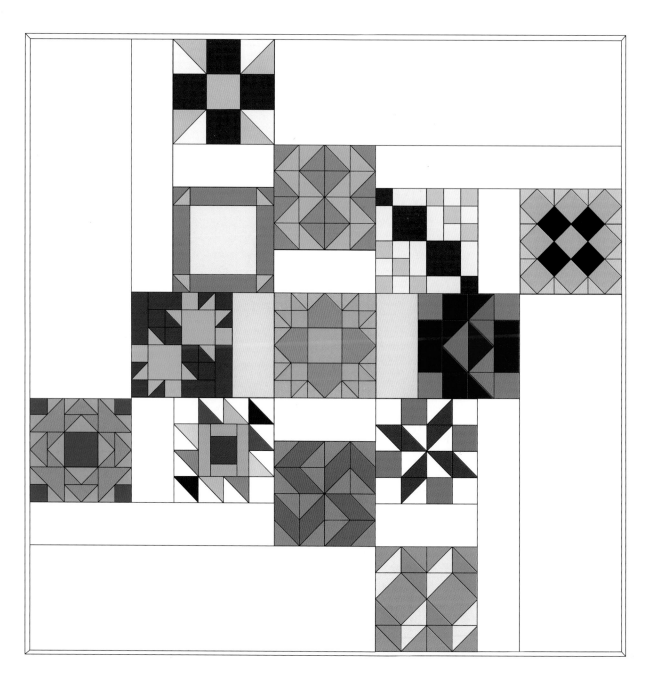

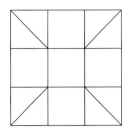
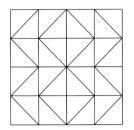
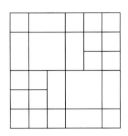

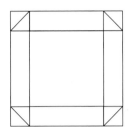
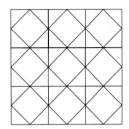

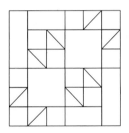
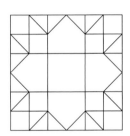
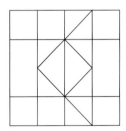

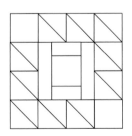
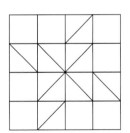

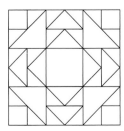
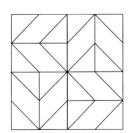
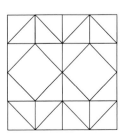

Sampler Setting

NO MATH GRID MEASUREMENTS

The measurements below were used to write instructions for blocks in this book. For each grid size I've calculated the number of squares in each grid and the finished size for each square within a 6, 9, and 12-inch finished quilt block. Based on the size of each square in a grid, I've included seam allowance to cut a square, half-square triangle, and quarter-square triangle. This is all the information you need to write instructions for or resize other blocks, or create your very own designs.

2 x 2 Grid
4 equal squares

		FINISHED BLOCK SIZE	4½"	6"	9"	12"
		GRID SQUARE SIZE	2¼ inch	3 inch	4½ inch	6 inch
add	½ inch	for square	2¾	3½	5	6½
add	⅞ inch	for HST	3⅛	3⅞	5⅜	6⅞
add	1¼ inch	for QST	3½	4¼	5¾	7¼

3 x 3 Grid
9 equal squares

		FINISHED BLOCK SIZE	4½"	6"	9"	12"
		GRID SQUARE SIZE	1½ inch	2 inch	3 inch	4 inch
add	½ inch	for square	2	2½	3½	4½
add	⅞ inch	for HST	2⅜	2⅞	3⅞	4⅞
add	1¼ inch	for QST	2¾	3¼	4¼	5¼

4 x 4 Grid
16 equal squares

		FINISHED BLOCK SIZE	4½"	6"	9"	12"
		GRID SQUARE SIZE	1⅛ inch	1½ inch	2¼ inch	3 inch
add	½ inch	for square	1⅝	2	2¾	3½
add	⅞ inch	for HST	2	2⅜	3⅛	3⅞
add	1¼ inch	for QST	2⅜	2¾	3½	4¼

5 x 5 Grid
25 equal squares

		FINISHED BLOCK SIZE	5"	10"	15"
		GRID SQUARE SIZE	1 inch	2 inch	3 inch
add	½ inch	for square	1½	2½	3½
add	⅞ inch	for HST	1⅞	2⅞	3⅞
add	1¼ inch	for QST	2¼	3¼	4¼

6 x 6 Grid
36 equal squares

		FINISHED BLOCK SIZE	4½"	6"	9"	12"
		GRID SQUARE SIZE	¾ inch	1 inch	1½ inch	2 inch
add	½ inch	for square	1¼	1½	2	2½
add	⅞ inch	for HST	1⅝	1⅞	2⅜	2⅞
add	1¼ inch	for QST	2	2¼	2¾	3¼

7 x 7 Grid
49 equal squares

		FINISHED BLOCK SIZE	7"	10½"	14"
		GRID SQUARE SIZE	1 inch	1½ inch	2 inch
add	½ inch	for square	1½	2	2½
add	⅞ inch	for HST	1⅞	2⅜	2⅞
add	1¼ inch	for QST	2¼	2¾	3¼

8 x 8 Grid
64 equal squares

		FINISHED BLOCK SIZE	8"	12"	16"
		GRID SQUARE SIZE	1 inch	1½ inch	2 inch
add	½ inch	for square	1½	2	2½
add	⅞ inch	for HST	1⅞	2⅜	2⅞
add	1¼ inch	for QST	2¼	2¾	3¼

No Math Grid Measurements

INCHES TO CM CHART

Inch	cm	Inch	cm	Inch	cm	Inch	cm
⅛"	0.32	5"	12.7	10"	25.40	15"	38.10
¼"	0.64	5⅛"	13.02	10⅛"	25.72	15⅛"	38.42
⅜"	0.95	5¼"	13.34	10¼"	26.04	15¼"	38.73
½"	1.27	5⅜"	13.65	10⅜"	26.35	15⅜"	39.10
⅝"	1.59	5½"	13.97	10½"	26.67	15½"	26.67
¾"	1.91	5⅝"	14.29	10⅝"	26.99	15⅝"	39.37
⅞"	2.22	5¾"	14.61	10¾"	27.31	15¾"	40.00
1"	2.54	5⅞"	14.92	10⅞"	27.62	15⅞"	40.32
1⅛"	2.86	6"	15.24	11"	27.94	16"	40.64
1¼"	3.18	6⅛"	15.56	11⅛"	28.26	16⅛"	41.00
1⅜"	3.49	6¼"	15.88	11¼"	28.58	16¼"	41.28
1½"	3.81	6⅜"	16.19	11⅜"	28.89	16⅜"	41.60
1⅝	4.13	6½"	16.51	11½"	29.21	16½"	41.91
1¾"	4.45	6⅝"	16.83	11⅝"	29.53	16⅝"	42.23
1⅞"	4.76	6¾"	17.15	11¾"	29.85	16¾"	42.54
2"	5.08	6⅞"	17.46	11⅞"	30.16	16⅞"	42.86
2⅛"	5.40	7"	17.78	12"	30.48		
2¼"	5.72	7⅛"	18.10	12⅛"	30.80		
2⅜"	6.03	7¼"	18.42	12¼"	31.12		
2½"	6.35	7⅜"	18.73	12⅜"	31.43		
2⅝"	6.67	7½"	19.05	12½"	31.75		
2¾"	6.99	7⅝"	19.37	12⅝"	32.07		
2⅞"	7.30	7¾"	19.68	12¾"	32.29		
3"	7.62	7⅞"	20.00	12⅞"	32.70		
3⅛"	7.94	8"	20.32	13"	33.02		
3¼"	8.26	8⅛"	20.64	13⅛"	33.34		
3⅜"	8.57	8¼"	20.96	13¼"	33.66		
3½"	8.89	8⅜"	21.27	13⅜"	34.00		
3⅝"	9.21	8½"	21.59	13½"	34.30		
3¾"	9.53	8⅝"	21.91	13⅝"	34.61		
3⅞"	9.84	8¾"	22.23	13¾"	35.00		
4"	10.16	8⅞"	22.54	13⅞"	35.24		
4⅛"	10.48	9"	22.86	14"	35.60		
4¼"	10.80	9⅛"	23.18	14⅛"	35.88		
4⅜"	11.11	9¼"	23.50	14¼"	36.20		
4½"	11.43	9⅜"	23.81	14⅜"	36.51		
4⅝"	11.87	9½"	24.13	14½"	36.83		
4¾"	12.07	9⅝"	24.45	14⅝"	37.14		
4⅞"	12.38	9¾"	24.77	14¾"	37.47		
		9⅞"	25.08	14⅞"	37.78		

BLOCK INDEX

BLOCK INDEX (continued)

BLOCK INDEX (continued

I've had so many opportunities in the past 14 years to meet talented quilt designers, photographing their amazing quilts, and keeping my eye on quilting trends while attending quilt markets. Thank you, Landauer authors, for your inspiration.

Penny Haren, you are the best! With your help, we started this block journey and I'm most appreciative of your knowledge and guidence.

To my workmate, friend, and designer extraordinare, Laurel Albright . . . it's been a great ride and so happy we will continue our work together.